ISBN 978-1-331-56358-7
PIBN 10206391

1 MONTH OF
FREE
READING

at
www.ForgottenBooks.com

By purchasing this book you are eligible for one month membership to ForgottenBooks.com, giving you unlimited access to our entire collection of over 700,000 titles via our web site and mobile apps.

To claim your free month visit:

www.forgottenbooks.com/free206391

RECOLLECTIONS

OF

SIXTY-THREE YEARS

OF

METHODIST LIFE

BY

THOMAS HAYES

𝕷𝖔𝖓𝖉𝖔𝖓:

PUBLISHED FOR THE AUTHOR

BY

CHARLES H. KELLY

25 AND 27, CITY ROAD, AND 26, PATERNOSTER ROW, E.C.

1902

PREFACE

SEVERAL of my friends have urged me to give to the public some of the recollections of my Methodist life. Whether they were wise in doing so, or whether I was wise in carrying out their suggestion, remains to be seen. When it was first hinted to me I quite ridiculed the idea of " writing a book," it seemed so preposterous. But the idea has clung to me, and the result is now given to the public with fear and trembling.

The late Dr. Punshon suggested to me, years ago, to write some of the memories of my life, for publication in the *Methodist Recorder*, of which at that time he was editor. I said in reply that I was sure I could write nothing that would be worth reading; but my judgment has been overruled, and, though I did not contribute anything to that influential journal during the editorship of Dr. Punshon, I have been an occasional contributor since, by the kindness of the Rev. Nehemiah Curnock, its present able and genial editor. Some of the jottings which have seen the light in the *Recorder* and in the *Wesleyan Methodist Church Record* will be found again in these pages, but the far greater part of the material appears for the first time.

THOMAS HAYES.

50 BROKE ROAD, DALSTON, N.E.,
October 1902.

———

_** On pages 20 and 22 it is stated that the Centenary Hall stood on the site of the old "London Tavern." This I find is an error. I should have said it was the "City of London Tavern." The old "London Tavern" stood on the opposite side in Bishopsgate Street, between Numbers 122 and 124. It was here that the historic meeting to found the Bible Society was held, early in 1804.

CONTENTS

RECOLLECTIONS OF SIXTY-THREE
YEARS OF METHODIST LIFE

——◆——

CHAPTER I

EARLY DAYS

I WAS born at Chelsea in 1824, "when George the Fourth was King." The days of my boyhood were stirring times, when political feeling ran high. Much disaffection both to monarch and Government was shown by the people, and the country was far from happy and prosperous. The working-man then had a very hard time: wages were low, every requisite of life was expensive and heavily taxed, travelling was difficult and costly, and could be indulged in only by those who were in easy circumstances, others being compelled to trudge afoot. Many years of war, chiefly with France, had added to our National Debt such a load as I suppose no country ever had to bear before. The population of London then was about one million six hundred thousand persons, about one-third of the number of those living to-day; and during my lifetime the area of London has increased to an extent commensurate with the increase of the population.

It is recorded that an American visiting London for the first time expressed himself as being greatly disappointed with the newness of everything. He said he had read of London as a place of importance in Roman, Saxon, and Norman times, but the place he saw was as new as New York. I can sympathise with this visitor, for it seems to me that I have seen almost half the metropolis built or rebuilt during my lifetime. Large districts which in the days of my boyhood were cornfields, meadows, gardens, and rural lanes, are now completely covered with houses.

The little section of north-east London where most of my life has been passed has shared in these changes. I have even now a vivid recollection of the orchards and fruit grounds which preceded the building of Broke Road, Dalston, where I live.

The manners and customs, too, of London have vastly changed since 1824. Think of London before Sir Robert Peel introduced the policeman (called after him "Peelers" or "Bobbies") being protected by a lot of feeble old watchmen. As a boy I have heard them, during the hours of darkness, droning out the time and the sort of weather it was —"Past two o'clock, and a cloudy morning." Who wanted to be awakened from sleep to receive this information ? It was one of the sports of our fast young men at that time to topple over the watchbox with the poor old Charley inside. Knocker-wrenching was also a fashionable sport with some of our young gentry. It is hard to realise now, but at that time prize-fighting and bull-baiting, as well as dog and cock-fighting, were unchecked by the authorities, and were vastly enjoyed by the rabble.

In these days of electric lighting it seems at times difficult to recall the London of my boyhood, when only the main thoroughfares were lighted by gas, and many of the smaller thoroughfares were lit up by oil lamps, which only served to make darkness visible. Many of the by-streets were regarded, and not without reason, as being too dangerous to be traversed by night. It is a little curious to note in London, however, how that the old and new are brought together; and a good illustration of this is now to be seen in Finsbury Square, where a house which is lighted by electric lamps has on its railings a large iron extinguisher into which the links carried by the footmen were thrust after " milord " and " milady " had gone indoors. In those early days Finsbury Square consisted of residences, not offices, as most of the houses now are. Then, again, the only way to get a light was by striking together flint and steel, and applying a brimstone match as soon as a spark struck the tinder. I have yet in my little museum part of the old family tinder-box which I used so often as a lad. These old-fashioned utensils, which were not considered worth preserving, are now valued as curiosities. In my very early boyhood I remember on one occasion I wanted to know the time, but, after striking with flint and steel in vain, through the tinder, I suppose, being damp, I sallied out from the house in the pitch-dark with my unlighted candle in hand, climbed up the nearest lamp-post, and obtained a light, to find on my return that it was three o'clock in the morning. We have certainly improved in our methods of getting a light.

The dashing of the Royal Mail coaches through London was then one of the sights of the metropolis. They were painted red, each drawn by four splendid horses, with coachman and guard in scarlet. Often have I waited at the corner of Kingsland Road, near Shoreditch Church, a few minutes after eight o'clock in the evening, to see four of the coaches rush past conveying the mails to the north of England. Railways, too, were very far from being general at that time. My first railway journey was to Folkestone before the station there was finished, and we had to alight by the side of the rails. On that journey the Parliamentary, or penny-a-mile, travellers had to travel in open trucks, exposed to steam, smoke, and weather. To call them carriages would be a misnomer. I have seen the Norwich and Norfolk coach at Christmas - time crammed inside and out with geese, turkeys, etc., for

Christmas fare, this load paying better than conveying passengers. At the same period of the year the large space in front of the Great Eastern Railway (then the Eastern Counties Railway) in Shoreditch, which was the headquarters before the grand station was built in Liverpool Street, was covered in with tarpaulins, crowded with counters and clerks and Christmas fare. It was a strange sight in the dark wintry days of Christmas.

The first London railway was the old Greenwich line, opened in 1836, when I was twelve years old. Omnibuses were first run in 1829. I remember a sort of steam omnibus running along part of City Road, and I remember, too, its coming to grief on entering the yard.

The death of George the Fourth took place in 1830, but I was then too young to attach much importance to it. The first event I do remember was the passing of the great Reform Bill in 1832, —not that I was at all interested in that important measure, but I recollect in connection with it that my brothers and I made small blocks of clay in which to stick the candles for the illumination which followed. I remember also that most of the houses were lighted up, and that the few which were left unilluminated had their windows smashed by people filled with patriotism, mischief, or drink, or all three in unholy combination. At the late Queen's Jubilee the Duke of Westminster suggested in the papers that this would be an appropriate and cheap method of showing our loyalty. I took the liberty of writing to tell His Grace that my brothers and I had done so those many years ago, and he courteously acknowledged my communication. The year 1834 was also marked by the burning of the Houses of Parliament, and I well remember watching the lurid sky on the evening of the fire. Then came the death of William the Fourth, when a general mourning was the fashion. This was followed by the accession of Her Majesty the late Queen Victoria, an event which seemed to inaugurate a general change. Old men had ruled us for long, and it was felt that young blood was wanted on the throne. In my humble judgment, it was the beginning of the most glorious reign in the history of the world, commencing so far back as 1837 and continuing to the year 1901. The changes for the better, which an observant person could not but notice, were really marvellous, but these have been so fully described by those who have written about our late beloved Queen that I need not dwell upon them. I may, however, be pardoned if for a moment I point out a few of the benefits which we now enjoy in comparison with the conditions prevailing in my boyhood. Then food was scarce and dear, clothing was costly, locomotion difficult, and literature the privilege of the few. Now we have abundance of excellent food; clothes and books are both good and cheap; and travel easy, comfortable, and inexpensive. Among the many other advantages we enjoy is that of cheap postage. In my early days at the Mission House Dr. Bunting gave me a letter to post to Manchester, which cost half-a-crown because there were two enclosures in it. Now it would go for one penny postage. Postage was a heavy charge on the Mission funds. Instead of being cooped up in single rooms in fetid alleys and courts, our working-men now can live out in the suburbs, using the trains specially run for them at almost nominal charges. Then, again, consider the sanitary laws by which we are governed. Here and there we still have foul spots and slums, but they are disappearing rapidly. In a few years, when the changes recently made have had time to take effect, many of our roads and open resorts will really be things of beauty; and I often think, in my own neighbourhood, of what the "London Fields" will be in years to come, when its fine avenues of trees have had time to grow. I remember how, even a few years ago, the graveyards of London suggested only feelings of gloom and desolation, but now they are being generally changed into pleasant gardens and places of recreation. We have a capital illustration of this change in the churchyard of our great Cathedral, where a very limited space has been so well turned to advantage.

I have a very vivid recollection of the period when the Chartists kept the well-behaved in a state of unrest. They were right in many of their demands, and these have since been granted; but they conducted their agitation in an improper way. Apropos of this Chartist time, I remember seeing the Bank of England with its top front wall piled up with sand-bags, which were arranged with loopholes for muskets, as a means of defence should the bank be attacked, as was expected. Crowds of people went to gaze upon the unwonted sight, many going away laughing at what they thought, and what turned out to be, unnecessary caution. Perhaps the Government took the matter more seriously than the public did.

Speaking of the Bank of England has recalled to me how that I remember a time when there stood on the space of ground where the Wellington Statue now stands, opposite the bank, a small block of houses used almost entirely by stockbrokers. The rents paid must have been a mine of wealth to the owner or owners. Many or all of the old-fashioned houses in Lombard Street have given place to splendid buildings. Banking houses, insurance companies, and stockbrokers are now the chief occupiers of that narrow but important street. I remember the Royal Exchange being burnt in 1838, and of my visiting it on my way home from the old Mission House in Hatton Garden. The fire took place during a very severe frost, and the long icicles formed by the freezing of the water pumped upon it by the firemen was a curious sight. The Poultry then was about half of its present width, so one may judge of the congested state it was often in. The opening of Queen Victoria Street, to relieve much of the Cheapside traffic, was a grand piece of work. The laying out and building of Cannon Street was a great undertaking. It seems to me also but a little while since that the north bank of the Thames between Westminster and Blackfriars was at low tide a filthy mud-bank, covered chiefly with barges laden with coal, and dotted over by wretched men and boys, known as mudlarks, who grubbed among the refuse for pieces of coal, scraps of iron, and fragments of metal. Now it is, in my judgment, one of the finest boulevards in Europe.

What shall be said of the Holborn Viaduct, formerly Holborn Hill? What a painful sight it was on a frosty day to see the horses prostrated as they endeavoured to climb the slippery hill! *Then* the entrance to St. Andrew's Church, where Wesley preached on February 12, 1738 (he adds to the entry in his Journal, " Here too, it seems, I am to preach no more "), was *up* a flight of steps. The neighbourhood of Farringdon Street, Smithfield, and other adjacent parts, have been improved during my lifetime almost beyond recognition. What a foul spot was the Fleet ditch, formerly the Fleet River, so called from its rapidity, along whose *silvery* stream, as old historians describe it, ships sailed to the Thames! I think I saw the last of the river when it was being bricked over and made the main sewer. I remember that I looked through the hoarding fronting it and thought of its history. This filthy stream, before it was covered in, was, in very heavy rain, a powerful body of water, carrying everything before it, as I have seen. It was made the receptacle of everything vile from the houses surrounding it.

Bartholomew Fair I have reason to remember, for it was there I lost my whole capital, a sum of seven shillings—all my savings at that period, and a fortune to me. Like many more, I must needs go through the fair instead of going about my business, as a good boy ought to have done, for I had but recently entered the Mission House service. I felt at the time that my loss was a judgment upon me. This fair, originally founded in A.D. 1133, and which during the fourteenth and fifteenth centuries was one of the most important in England, had become, at the time of my recollection, a scene of riotous amusement and dissipation, and the question of its abolition had been discussed for many years. There were, however, certain vested rights attached to it; and such rights die hard. It was removed in 1840 to Islington, and finally suppressed in 1855. The cattle-market at Smithfield was also a famous sight: the noise, the shouting and yelling of the drivers, the bellowing of the cattle, the bleating of the sheep, and the squealing of the pigs may give one an idea of what Smithfield Market was in its glory. I have passed along the footways and had to push aside the horns of the cattle to get along, the path being so narrow. One of Punch's cartoons in those days represented a fat alderman walking with his family in Smithfield, descanting on the rich odours of the place, the drains, etc. In time, however, when the market was removed, I saw that a pretty little paradise, with trees, flowers, etc., with seats for wayfarers, had actually been laid out in the centre spot of the old market.

Farringdon Road, before it was laid out and built, was a labyrinth of cross-roads, streets, and alleys. One alley, I remember, had the queer name of " Frying-Pan Alley." It was a vile slum, which I should not have ventured to enter alone. This, with many more like it, was swept away for the new road. In this wide road sometimes as many as fifty bookstalls may now be counted. It is a veritable book-market. Needless to say, I know the spot well.

I call to mind Wilderness Row with its old Methodist Chapel, built back as though afraid of being seen. It forms part of the new road just spoken of. This chapel was the precursor of the St. John's Square place of worship. The Charterhouse School, where Wesley partly received his education, stood on the southern side of the " Row." This new road, with its excellent service of trams, now connects the west with the north of the great metropolis.

I must not omit another feature of the old London of my boyhood, namely the parish crier or bellman, whose business it was to announce parish notices. Often as a lad have I stopped to hear him tell the lookers-on, in a monotonous voice, a list of parish meetings and other matters. On one occasion I heard a crier winding up his announcements thus, "And to take into consideration the repair of the parish pump," with tremendous emphasis on the last word.

The well-known crimes of Burke and Hare in Edinburgh had their counterpart also in London, and in my earlier days after dark I used to hurry past a certain garden in the East End of London, where a poor Italian boy had been murdered for the value of his dead body. For many years, too, graves were robbed of their occupants, in order that the bodies might be used in the medical schools. The men who carried on this vile trade were known as resurrectionists. The practice was brought to an end by an Act of Parliament passed in 1832.

Early in my life my parents removed to the neighbourhood of St. Pancras, and there several years of my boyhood were spent. Then, country lanes and quiet roads were the chief features of the district, but this neighbourhood has seen, perhaps, as great changes as any part of the metropolis. The huge station of the Great Northern Railway stands on a large space of ground formerly occupied by a large fever hospital. This station, as regards its exterior, is often described as the ugliest in London. Possibly its want of beauty is the more striking, inasmuch as the neighbouring one of the Midland Railway is one of the finest we have. Very many dwellings were pulled down and cleared away to make room for the latter stately building.

It would be easy to continue these rambling recollections of the alterations I have observed in the streets and buildings of the metropolis, but considerations of time and space forbid. The many changes I have seen, however, have often carried me back in imagination to the period when our rude forefathers lived in huts like wigwams, or in caves and hollows scooped out of the earth on the banks of our river, and when the only way to cross it was by floating log or dug-out canoe. Then, the deep ravine of the Fleet protected the inhabitants on the west, the rushing Walbrook on the east; behind them was the great forest with its savage beasts; before them was the Thames, spreading far and wide over what was then the lakes and marshes of Lambeth and Southwark. It seems almost impossible to imagine that this was the beginning of our mighty London, with its five millions of inhabitants, its myriads of buildings, and its world-wide fame; but there is every reason to believe that such was the case.

CHAPTER II

INTRODUCTION TO THE OLD WESLEYAN
MISSION HOUSE

IT was in 1837, when I was nearly fourteen years of age, that I was engaged as office-boy at the old Mission House in Hatton Garden. My going there arose from what at the time seemed to be a very trifling circumstance, but to me it was an important event, for it was the beginning of my Methodist life, and I have always regarded it as most providential. It was thus: The accountant of the Mission House then was Mr. John Wesley, grandson of the Rev. Charles Wesley, the Poet of Methodism, and one of his female relatives lodged in the house occupied by my parents. Hearing that an office-boy was wanted at the Mission House, she introduced me to Mr. Wesley, who, being satisfied with the answers I gave to his questions, told me to call next day and see the house secretary, Mr. Alder; which I did. After sundry questions, and I suppose satisfactory answers, I was engaged for a month on trial. I little thought then that my " trial " would last forty-five years; but it was in that way there came about that which shaped my whole life.

I do not propose writing a history of our Missions, for that has been well done by others—notably by the late venerable William Moister, a missionary to the backbone, and but recently by the Rev. John Telford, whose popular summary of the Society's operations is a marvel of compactness. The old *Missionary Notices*, too, form a choice storehouse of missionary information, and afford abundance of interesting matter for the friends of Missions. The Annual Reports, also, form admirable summaries of the work of each year.

In earlier days of Methodist history the burden of our Missions rested for many years on Dr. Coke, who was superintendent, treasurer, collector, and general manager of our Missionary Society. At his departure for India, in 1814—which distant place, however, he did not reach, being found dead in his cabin on the voyage out—the Society was reorganised, and in the course of a few years placed on its present permanent footing. In 1816 it was decided to rent two rooms for the use of the Society at No. 4 City Road, and at the following Conference a house was taken in Hatton Garden, No. 77, which was afterwards purchased, to be its headquarters. Hatton Garden took its name from Sir Christopher Hatton, the Chancellor and favourite of Queen Elizabeth, and it formed part of the Hatton House estate. It was to the old Mission

House that Joseph Taylor came as the first official Missionary Secretary, although he had in addition to perform the usual Circuit work. He had been for eight years a missionary in the West Indies, and I can readily recall to remembrance the appearance of this venerable gentleman after he had resigned his secretaryship, but still came as a member of the Missionary Committee to Hatton Garden. He was very sedate in his manner; and in his old-fashioned, almost Quaker-like, dress he always seemed to me the *beau ideal* of the early Methodist preacher. The old Mission House had been a private dwelling, as, in fact, all the houses were in Hatton Garden when first built. Now every house is a business place, chiefly occupied by watchmakers, jewellers, diamond merchants, etc. The Rev. Edward Irving, at one time very celebrated, held his services in a small chapel opposite the Mission House. The house in time became too crowded for comfort, as the work increased every year. The front room on the ground floor was the clerks' office, and was occupied then by the book-keeper, Mr. North (who died in the jubilee year of his service); the accountant, Mr. Wesley; the shipping clerk, Mr. King, soon succeeded by the late Mr. Samuel Adams; and the office-boy. Mr. W. T. Brown, clerk and copyist, who had also charge of the missionaries' correspondence, afterwards went to Spain as one of the Society's agents. The back parlour, as it may be termed, was occupied by Mr. Hoole and Dr. Bunting, the first floor back room by Mr. Beecham, and the second floor by Mr. Alder. The most important room was that used by the Missionary Committee; it was the front room on the first floor, and, though the largest in the house, was oftentimes inconveniently crowded.

It was during these meetings that I began to notice with interest some of our grand old men, and, as I write, visions of the stately Richard Reece, who entered the ministry in 1787 and ended it in 1850, come before me. Then George Marsden, of whom it was said that he was never seen to laugh but once, when something comical was said of one of the preachers; I don't think, though I saw him many times, that I ever saw him smile. William Atherton, Joseph Entwisle, Theophilus Lessey, William Naylor (who preached sermons on the formation of the Society and at its jubilee), Edmund Grindrod, Dr. Newton, Thomas and Samuel Jackson, with many more. I saw but once or twice the venerable Henry Moore. What a galaxy of grand old men! Methodism clings to the memory of her old preachers, and, as time passes on, that feeling increases. One may say there were giants in those days, but let us acknowledge also we have giants to-day. The treasurers then were Mr. Thomas Farmer and the Rev. John Scott. I still prize a book Mr. Farmer gave me, with an inscription. With Mr. Scott I was somewhat of a favourite. May I be forgiven

if I mention that one of his daughters told me
on one occasion that her father advised her and
her sister to take "Thomas" as a pattern of dili-
gence, etc.   This put me to the blush, and I
made a low bow, remarking that it was too
flattering.

CHAPTER III

THE CENTENARY HALL

THE Mission House in Bishopsgate Street, perhaps better known as the Centenary Hall, was
purchased out of the Centenary Fund for fifteen
thousand pounds, and about the same amount was
expended in alteration and rebuilding. The saloon
and committee-room, with the large room at the
top of the building, were left untouched, with the
exception of the decorations. The back part of
the house was entirely rebuilt. The front had a
very imposing proportion, but the house narrowed
considerably at the back, the rear not being more
than half the width of the front. I little thought,
when I occasionally went from Hatton Garden to
watch its progress, that I should live to see its
very foundations laid bare, as I did a few months
ago. I hope I may live to see it rebuilt, and
in use as a vastly improved erection. There
certainly was room for great improvement, for in
the old building much valuable space was lost.
Land has increased enormously in value within
the City boundaries since the Centenary Hall was

built, and it is now a matter of moment that every square yard of space should be used to advantage. Even the spaces below, formerly devoted to cellarage, are now by the aid of prisms and reflectors made available for offices.

The Centenary Hall and Mission House was opened in January 1841, with sermons by Dr. Bunting, Dr. Newton, and the venerable Richard Reece. Well do I remember the day we took possession,—how I ran into all the rooms of the house that I might see the great change we had made, and how I was impressed by the grandeur of the new building. It certainly was a splendid house; the builder had left it in prime condition, and the paint-work was of the best. One thing impressed me at the time: the British and Foreign Bible Society, with their usual generosity, had made our New Zealand Mission a grant of 5000 New Testaments for the use of the natives of that colony, and the men from the Bible house were busy packing them for shipment. I thought this was a noble form of dedication of the new house.

Many people came to see the Hall, and were very pleased with it. Outside the " Old London Tavern," its former name, was a massive coat-of-arms of the City; this was fixed in a niche in the large room, and was the only alteration made in it. The orchestra for the musicians was turned into a gallery. A platform was erected for speakers, and a pulpit for preachers. Each end of the room was filled with looking-glass in shape of windows, which in a good light gave the strange sight of an endless perspective. For many years the President for the time being preached one of the missionary sermons in this room, and many ordinations of missionaries took place; but its great ascent prevented its general use. I don't suppose that such a room would have been erected; but, as it formed part of the building, and was thought that it would be useful for meetings, services, etc., it was suffered to remain. One of its early uses was the holding of a very large bazaar for the sale of a ship-load of South Sea curiosities, and it was a very successful one. This was not the only missionary bazaar held there. The Jewin Street congregation worshipped there while their chapel was building. Many Connexional gatherings took place within its walls; and the Young Men's Christian Association commenced their famous lectures there, alternating with the Freemasons' Tavern in Great Queen Street.

The old building had a history of its own. For balls and other festive gatherings it was always in request. It was much used by the various philanthropical societies for their annual meetings, etc. Very early last century a meeting was called here for the purpose of establishing the British and Foreign Bible Society. Its good dinners and festivities in time came to an end, when the New London Tavern, nearly opposite, was opened. This was during the Centenary year, and among the schemes to be carried out by that Fund was the erection of a Mission House worthy of the Society and monumental of the Centenary of Methodism. By a strange coincidence, the Old London Tavern was at that time in the market for sale. After deep and anxious deliberation, the Centenary Fund Committee determined to purchase the building and the value of this purchase for fifteen thousand pounds has risen, during just over sixty years, to a quarter of a million sterling.

The corner of Threadneedle Street facing the Mission House has of late been greatly widened; formerly there stood an old church, St. Martin's Outwych, the rector of which had a very good " living," if nothing to do and being well paid constituted it a good " living." He well looked after his tithes, which we, with other neighbours, had to pay, while he let out the parsonage next door to his church for offices. He paid a curate to look after about a dozen attendants. At the opposite corner the National and Provincial Bank stands on the site of an old inn, the " Flower Pot," where omnibuses for Kingsland and other parts north took their departure. My brother-in-law, James Wilkinson, was clerk of works at the building of this magnificent bank, as well as the almost rebuilding of Mercers' Hall in the Poultry, the City Temple, the Scottish Bank, and other large buildings. The City Bank (now the City and County Bank) began business in my time at the corner of Finch Lane in Threadneedle Street, with a very small staff of clerks; now it employs a small army. The same may be said of the "Star Life Assurance Company," showing that these businesses have met with marvellous success. The number of my "Life" Policy in the "Star" is 126,—showing that I was an early member. At the end of June 1902 the last Policy issued was No. 117,495. This speaks for itself.

CHAPTER IV

THE MISSION HOUSE MUSEUM

NOW that the Centenary Hall has passed away, a brief description of it may not be without interest. The saloon and committee - room on the first floor were not structurally altered, as before stated. In the saloon was safely housed a collection of missionary relics and the Connexional museum. The nucleus of the former came from Hatton Garden, but has been largely expanded, mainly through the generosity of Mr. and Mrs. H. J. Farmer-Atkinson. The late Mr. Thomas Farmer, of Gunnersbury House, was one of the best helpers of our missionaries and their work, and was constantly receiving gifts of rare and curious articles, natural, ethnological, and religious, from his grateful friends on the Mission field. These came into the possession of his son-in-law, Mr. Farmer-Atkinson, and were in course of time transferred to the custody of the Mission House. It was a grand gift, and found in the Mission House saloon a worthy home. It requires a well-written handbook to set forth the value and interest of such a choice collection. This noble gift was quite in keeping with the princely generosity of Mr. and Mrs. Atkinson.

In the saloon there hung the famous painting of John Wesley's deathbed scene, by Marshall Claxton. It represents the aged saint dying in a room of noble proportions, surrounded by about a dozen of his intimate friends. When I first saw the room which tradition says was the death-chamber, I remarked that surely could not be the case, that Mr Wesley could not have ended his life in such a small room. I believe that, when he or his friends felt the end was coming, he was taken into the front room on the same floor, and there he breathed out his life. This room was larger and more cheerful, affording better space for air and attendance. One of our best anti-quarians, the Rev. Nehemiah Curnock, told me that he concurred with me in this opinion. It is strange that no record is known to exist giving precise information on this point. Elizabeth Ritchie, immediately after the death, published an account of the last fortnight of Mr. Wesley's life, but said nothing as to the room. A single stroke of her pen, almost, would have set at rest an interesting question. The painting is a fine bit of skill, and the figures are well grouped. Those who possess the engraving will agree with me that it is quite a study. One of the figures has his face buried in his handkerchief: this was Mr. Horton, one of

Wesley's dear friends. As there was no known portrait, the artist has so represented him. In looking at this picture, I have thought how few links are required to connect long periods of time. The boy shown here is the one link joining two hundred years, thus : John Wesley was born in 1703, and no doubt sometimes spoke kindly to the boy, giving him his blessing, etc., he being the son of James and Hester Ann Rogers, who lived in the City Road house, and who in his old age has often spoken to me, thus joining two centuries, for I am writing this in 1902. I suppose tradition was handed down in this way. The painting had been bought at a picture sale, and the owner asked permission to exhibit it at the Mission House, with the hope of disposing of it. I set my mind on the picture, and cast about how it might be secured. On talking with Dr. Hoole, he suggested that I should try to collect the price asked for it—eighty pounds. I gladly undertook to do this, and succeeded, and formally presented it to the Committee, through the Rev. Luke H. Wiseman, and it was duly entered in the Minute Book of the Committee. There is also a valuable painting of John Wesley, by Williams, a well-known artist in the early part of the eighteenth century. It may be regarded as the first portrait of John Wesley. I saw it at an old picture shop in Jewin Street, priced at five guineas. Dr. Hoole greatly admired it, as also did Dr. Jobson —no mean artist. It was cleaned and framed. I

suppose a dealer now would ask a hundred pounds
for it. The securing of these two valuable paint-
ings is always a source of pleasure to me. Here,
perhaps, is the best place to tell another picture
tale. Very many years ago a person brought to
the Mission House a three-quarter-length painting
of what he was told to be Mrs. Susannah Wesley,
for which he wanted ten pounds. On showing
the picture to the Rev. William Arthur, who was
then one of the Missionary Secretaries, he suggested
that I should write to the late Mr. George Morley,
of Leeds, which I did. He replied that he would
gladly take it if the vendor could give a guarantee
that it was a portrait of Mrs. Wesley. This the
person offering it could not do. Strange to say, he
afterwards met with sufficient evidence to satisfy
Mr. Morley, who sent me the price asked. The
painting now forms one of the treasures of
Headingley College.

I must not omit the grand painting of the
rescue of John Wesley when a child from the
fire at Epworth. It was painted by Mr. H. P.
Parker, and was his gift to the Wesleyan Centenary
Fund. Many of the portraits on the walls of
the saloon and committee - room are of special
interest—that of John Wesley's wife, Mrs. Vazaille,
being noteworthy. It is the only one known.
Another lady's portrait must not be overlooked—
that of Mrs. Jones, afterwards Mrs. Hincksman,
the sole survivor of the disastrous wreck of the

Maria mail-boat, in 1826. The tale of this wreck is a missionary classic, and has often been read. She tells in her deeply affecting narrative how she held her dying husband in her arms till her strength was exhausted and he was washed away. The portrait of good William Smith, of Gledhow, the founder of the Headingley Missionary Breakfast, also that of George Royle Chappell, a staunch Manchester supporter of Methodist Missions, occupied prominent positions on the walls. Such men ought never to die. There are also fine portraits of John Sunday, Peter Jones, and Peter Jacobs, representing the success of Methodist work among the North American Indians; also those of John Gaulter (President in 1817), Dr. Hoole, Mr. Perks, Mr. Wiseman, Dr. Waddy, Dr. Punshon, and many more. The busts included Mr. Farmer, Dr. Newton, George Morley (father of the Leeds Methodist antiquarian), Richard Watson, Dr. Bunting, Dr. Beecham, Mr. James Heald, and others. There was also a beautiful replica, reduced in size, of Mr. Acton Adams's fine bronze statue in front of Wesley's Chapel.

"The Museum of Methodist Antiquities" was originated by Dr. Jobson and Dr. Punshon. Mr. M'Naughton's legacy to the Conference, part of which was directed to be appropriated to such a purpose, gave the movement a beginning. Later, the gifts of loving and reverent Methodists in all parts of the country made it necessary to provide large flat show-cases, which were placed beneath the windows of the saloon. In the corner case, among other treasures, were thirty quarto volumes of letters and portraits of Wesleyan ministers, bequeathed by the late Mr. William Bourne, who may almost be regarded as the first collector of such literature. I had the pleasure of helping him to many items of Methodist interest. Being so early in the field, he had opportunities for collecting which he would not have now had he lived. In these flat show-cases were interesting letters of John Wesley, John Fletcher, Dr. Coke, George Whitefield, and one from the notorious Dr. Dodd to Miss Bosanquet, afterwards Mrs. Fletcher, commencing, " On Friday next I am to be made immortal. I die with a heart broken by its manifold transgressions," etc. It is a most repentant letter. In the same case was a portion of Susannah Wesley's beautifully neat handwriting, dated " From the Foundery, July 1, 1741." A remarkable feature of the Wesley family is the beautiful handwriting shown by all its members. There are many interesting Wesley relics; also a copy of the quarto edition of Wesley's Notes on the New Testament, with marginal notes written by Mr. Toplady, whose bitter feeling towards Mr. Wesley is shown in these MS. notes. For many years I had charge of the Mission House museum, and it tended to increase my knowledge of and interest in

Methodist antiquities.   I fear, however, that I am wearying my readers by these details.   I doubt not but that the new Mission House will have a room worthy the reception of such a collection.

CHAPTER V

THAT portion of my life spent at the Mission House covers a period of forty-five years, and I have been looking through the *Missionary Notices* for those years to refresh my memory with the incidents recorded, many of them, however, being but slightly referred to.

1837

Our Theological Institution at Hoxton was originally a large private residence, as many of the houses in Hoxton were in former days. In the seventeenth century numbers of the nobility lived there, each house standing in its own grounds. It was at his residence in Hoxton that Lord Monteagle received the mysterious letter which led to the discovery of the infamous Gunpowder Plot. All these fine old houses have disappeared, some of them in my time.

The College had the honour of preparing for their work some of the best missionaries which the Society has sent into the Mission field, among whom may be mentioned John Hunt, James Calvert, and William Arthur. The Wesleyan Chapel in Hackney Road, known then as Middlesex Chapel, often had a student in its pulpit, those I have just named being among them. The College becoming after a time too small, Abney House, Stoke Newington, was engaged; and the associations of this mansion are deeply interesting, the worthy Sir Thomas Abney and his world-known guest, Dr. Isaac Watts, giving to the house a choice memory.

The earliest note of interest this year was that of the Government having made a grant of £2000 for native schoolhouses for the Fingoes of Kaffraria who had been emancipated from slavery. The Committee placed a missionary in their midst. The case of Kama and his people was of deep interest. The chief and his officials met in council, and earnestly pleaded that they could not live without a missionary, whom the Kaffirs regarded as their best and truest friend—an estimate fully justified by the long years of cheerful sacrifice and of patient labour which the missionaries had given for their spiritual and temporal welfare.

The connection of the East India Company with idolatry in India had become by this time a public scandal, and the Company was at last compelled to give way, but it was a tardy concession. It was reputed that the receipts from the Juggernaut and other temples were not less than £10,000 annually, while Hindu Christians were compelled to drag the car of the hideous idol. For a long time there was a tradition among the superstitious natives of India, to the effect that whoever possessed the Dadala Relic, or Tooth of Buddha, would be ruler of the land; and the East Indian Government fostered the superstition, the relic being kept in the custody of its Commissioner, and brought out at stated intervals for worship. But the rule of "John Company" came to an end before many years in spite of its Dadala Relic.

To Dr. Lindoe and his friends at Southampton the Foulah Mission in West Africa was greatly indebted. Truly we have had men who loved their brothers though black in colour; and good Dr. Lindoe was one, with a host of others who might be named.

The Lieutenant-Governor of Jamaica this year in the Legislative Assembly spoke of the importance and necessity of missionary labour to prepare the negro population for their entire freedom—a contrast to the earlier days of our Mission in Jamaica, when missionaries were brutally ill-used, chapels pulled down, and other ill deeds were done by the planters and others.

Good Sir Andrew Agnew, who presided at the Missionary Meeting this year, was one of the most earnest advocates for the observance of the Sabbath, and I can remember how he used to be caricatured by his opponents.

1838

The departure this year of John Hunt, James Calvert, and T. J. Jaggar for Fiji (formerly spelt Feejee), was an important event in our Mission history. Not that the going forth of a small party of young missionaries to their distant appointment was of a specially noteworthy character, but in this case it helped to bring about marvellous results. Mr. Hunt was a prince of missionaries, and, precious as his life was, it was comparatively a short one— from 1838 to 1848. He died pleading for Fiji. An interesting Memoir of him was written by the Rev. G. Stringer Rowe. Mr. Calvert lived to a good old age, dying forty - four years after his brother-missionary. Who does not call to mind his homely, ruddy face? I am proud to be reckoned among his friends.

Late in 1838 an event occurred which greatly grieved the Committee—in fact, all Missionary Methodism—in the death of Mr. and Mrs. Peard (recently married) by shipwreck, during a terrible storm off Weymouth, in which the *Columbine*, with all on board, was lost. She was on her way to Sierra Leone. Mr. Alder, then one of the Missionary Secretaries, with whom Mr. and Mrs. Peard stayed previous to their embarking, went to Weymouth to identify their bodies should they be washed ashore. Mr. Peard's body was recovered, and interred in the burial - ground attached to

Portland Chapel, Mr. Alder preaching to a deeply affected congregation. Mrs. Peard's body was soon after found, and placed in the same grave. Such was the violence of the storm that but a small plane and a stocking, with Mr. Peard's name on them, were recovered. Nine other vessels were in the same storm, with great loss of life. Those early years were sad times for our West African Missions; one missionary after another being carried off by fever, some after a very brief career. The arrival of the West Coast mails, I remember, used to be a time of great anxiety. These Missions were in charge of Mr. Beecham, whom I greatly respected. A thorough gentleman, he was very stately in his manner, but very kind. His valuable and interesting book, *Ashantee and the Gold Coast*, showed his deep interest in those Missions. He was one among a number of large-minded philanthropists to whom the aborigines of various countries owed much. His colleague, Dr. Hoole, wrote an interesting Memoir of him in the *Methodist Magazine* for 1856.

This year it is recorded that a party of native teachers, including Joel Bulu, went to Fiji to reinforce the Mission there, which was commenced by Messrs. Cross and Cargill in 1835; this field of missionary labour, by a wise and mutual arrangement with the Directors of the London Missionary Society, being left to our Society's agents. Joel Bulu spent many years as a native missionary, dying in 1877, and was buried beside his old friend, John Hunt. King Thakombau, who had been a fierce cannibal in earlier life, had embraced Christianity, and made Joel Bulu his chaplain, and he with his family followed the native missionary to his grave. Think of a cannibal king in course of time possessing a Christian chaplain! A printing-press was among the benefits conferred on the Fijian Mission, and it was a wonderful help to our agents. Before missionaries went to Fiji, I have read that at a single feast three hundred men and women were killed and eaten. Among the items in the Mission House museum was a little tract of a few leaves, in which Mr. Cargill had written that it was the first book printed in Fiji. I regarded it with great interest, and gave it good prominence.

Later in this year a party of six missionaries were wrecked fifty-seven miles from Madras, but passengers and crew were all saved. One of the missionaries and the ship's surgeon travelled for two days before help could be had. Mr. and Mrs. Moister, with four other missionaries, just after leaving St. Vincent, in the West Indies, were wrecked on a coral reef, and in one short hour their vessel was completely dashed to pieces, but without loss of life.

At the Exeter Hall Meeting, Mr. Bumby, appointed to New Zealand, spoke with telling effect. He told how his friends urged him to stay at home, but

He heard a voice they did not hear,
He saw a hand they could not see.

His tragic death by drowning soon after his arrival in New Zealand was deeply felt. The deaths of seven missionaries' wives, in some cases leaving children, were recorded this year, and these events cast a gloom over the many friends of the Society.

This year the Earl Fitzwilliam and his family gave a contribution of £50 to the Society's funds.

1839

This year the Missionary Committee determined to purchase a ship for the use of the South Sea Missions, out of the Centenary Fund; and a small sailing-ship, the *Triton*, was secured. It was of 120 tons burden, a truly small affair for a voyage of 20,000 miles, and for such work. I well remember what a busy time it was, receiving stores, etc., for the ship, and for the missionaries in the far-off southern world. Many of the supporters of the Missionary Society in those days gave handsome gifts in kind as well as money. So many offerings came to hand that many of them had to be shipped to Sydney by another vessel. It was also found that the *Triton* was unable to accommodate the large party of missionaries going out, and they had to follow by another ship. The *Triton*, however, was fully loaded, and carried provisions for twelve months. It was high time that better provision should be made for the comfort of the missionaries. Some of the distant islands were seldom visited, and

often weary months passed without the sight of a
ship, and the mission families, having consumed
their little store, had to depend upon the gifts of
the natives and live upon native fare. The departure of the *Triton* was delayed for nearly a
fortnight, owing to the captain waiting for a
favourable wind. Our shipping arrangements have
changed greatly for the better since then.

The Anniversary Collections this year realised the
large sum of £2643, which I think worth recording. The year's income was £4795 above the
expenditure, to the great joy of the Committee,
and in fact all at the Mission House. But at the
same time a debt of £20,000 had accumulated,
which greatly hindered the Society's operations.

It was in this year that the Rev. William Arthur
went to India to reinforce the Mysore Mission. I
shall refer to him later on. Another remarkable
man whom I call to mind was Peter Jones, a grand-
looking North American Indian chief, fully six
feet high, by whose visit to England deep interest
was awakened in the natives of North America.
He was the first Ojibeway Indian who became a
minister of the gospel, and during a period of
thirty years led a life remarkable for piety and usefulness. When I saw him he had been honoured
with audiences by two British sovereigns. Another
American Indian, John Sunday, with an equally
grand presence, was a visitor to England, and spoke
at many missionary meetings.

The name of Thomas B. Freeman at this time was in almost everybody's mouth. His "Journal," recording his travels to Ashantee, was one of the most interesting missionary books written. It led to the establishment of a Mission there. This, of course, was many years after our war with the Ashantees, in which our troops under Sir Charles Macarthy suffered defeat, he being slain. The victors cut off his head, and made of the skull a drinking-cup. Notwithstanding the Society's heavy debt, just named, a special fund was opened for the Ashantee Mission, headed, as a matter of course, by our munificent treasurer, Mr. Farmer.

What a contrast is afforded by the travelling and voyaging of the missionaries in those early days with the present! No splendid steamships, as now, making their voyages in about one-fourth of the time formerly taken. With very rare exceptions, we have not had a shipwrecked missionary for many years. Generally the ships formerly used were small traders only, and the result was often shipwreck and disaster and death, including the before-named Mr. and Mrs. Peard, also Mrs. Fleet, whose sufferings during that same fatal storm caused her death before she reached Sierra Leone. Peter Jones, too, lost all from the same cause; as did also Mr. Longbottom and Mr. Cross, in the South Seas. What courage and devotion have in numberless cases been shown by our missionaries and by their wives! Surely their record is on high.

Much labour was expended and very much prayer offered for Fiji, cannibal Fiji, and glorious was the result vouchsafed by the Almighty, for in time, comparatively a short time, the islands became almost entirely Christianised. What joy this was to the missionaries who had laboured so earnestly there! One must read the history of the Fijian Mission, to realise the great change which within my memory has taken place in these islands. It is an almost literal fulfilment of the promise that a nation shall be born in a day.

Miss Gordon-Cumming, in her deeply interesting work, *Our Home in Fiji*, written years after this period, was delighted with what she saw there. She wrote: "The first sound which greets your ear at dawn, and the last at night, is that of hymn-singing and fervent worship, arising from each dwelling at the hour of family prayer. Doors are left open while the people are at the service, without fear of theft. Every family in the eighty inhabited islands begins and ends the day with singing Christian hymns, and reading the Scriptures, and prayers."

Mr. William Dawson, the grand old Yorkshire farmer, having placed himself at the service of the Missionary Committee, a fund was raised for his support and invested in the purchase of an annuity. The sum was invested in the Missionary Society, which in time fell into their hands. "Billy Dawson," as he was familiarly called, preached with

power, and was long remembered. His " Telescope "
speech was a masterpiece of eloquence.[1]   I heard
him preach at City Road Chapel on " God so loved
the world." Altogether, this year was a remarkable
one.

1840

Early this year King George of Tonga, who
had embraced Christianity, promulgated a code
of laws which was an honour to him and to
the missionaries by whom he had been instructed.
The preamble is worth quoting in its English
translation. " I, George, make known this my
mind to the chiefs of the different parts of
Haafuluhao, also to all my people. May you
be very happy ! It is of the God of heaven and
earth that I have been appointed to speak to you.
He is King of kings and Lord of lords. He doeth
whatsoever He pleaseth. He lifteth up one and
putteth down another. He is righteous in all His
works. We are all the work of His hands and the
sheep of His pasture, and His will towards us
is that we should be happy. Therefore it is that
I make known to you all, to the chiefs and
governors and people, as well as the different
strangers and foreigners that live with me," etc.
Then follow a series of laws highly conducive

[1] The resolution he had to move was rolled up into the form of
a telescope, and what he saw in imagination of the success of
missionary work was splendidly described.

to the welfare of the people. The king was a trophy of missionary labour.

The officials of the old East India Company, a very powerful corporation at this period, were greatly opposed to missionary work in India, protecting, if not patronising, many of the idolatrous festivals—notably that of Juggernaut. At the Annual Meeting at Exeter Hall Dr. Dixon moved a strong resolution to the effect that the Government of Madras should be petitioned against its sanction of idolatry in India. The East India Company, as is well known, ceased to exist soon after the Sepoy rebellion, and India became, what it ought to have been long before, one of the dependencies of Great Britain.

The Mission to Ashantee had now been taken up by the Society, and the arrival of Mr. Freeman, its pioneer, gave interest to it. He spoke at many missionary meetings, and at the end of the year returned to the scene of his labours with a large reinforcement of helpers. The party were dismissed from our shores with intense feelings of interest and with much prayer.

Much sympathy at this period was being felt for the "Red Men of the Far West," who had suffered much from the conduct of the white men towards them. A brighter day began to dawn upon the remnant that was left, and sympathy was awakened on their behalf. In the Governor of Hudson's Bay the Indian Missions in Canada found a real friend; and five missionaries were appointed to labour in various parts of that immense tract of land. The Company greatly assisted in this noble work, in marked contrast to the doings of the East India Company just named. One of the best friends the Cree Indians had was the Rev. James Evans, who had charge of that Mission. A noteworthy result of his labours was the invention of the Cree syllabic character.

We were occasionally favoured in those early days with visits from some of the Colonial Governors, most of whom took a deep interest in our Missions. Among them I remember Governor Maclean of Cape Coast, the husband of the gifted Miss Landon, better known by her initials of L. E. L.; also Sir George Simpson, Governor of Hudson's Bay; also the Governor of the Gambia. The names of others have escaped my memory.

1841

Soon after the year commenced, Dr. Enoch Wood told us of a most destructive fire which had taken place at St. John, New Brunswick, and which had destroyed property of the value of £35,000. The Wesleyan Chapel was the last building consumed. Dr. Wood was the Society's Superintendent of Missions in Canada. He entered the ministry in 1826, and had spent a large part of his private fortune in the work. He was an occasional visitor to the Mission House, and was much attached to me, while I really loved him. He made me his agent for the purchase of books, and many pounds passed between us in this way.

Good old Ralph Stott, of the Ceylon Mission, reported this year a great religious awakening among the Veddahs, or Wild Men of the Jungle, of whom a great number received Christian baptism. These were sincere converts, and their baptism was altogether unlike that of which I have read somewhere, when the Jesuit missionaries scattered the water wholesale over the crowds of people, and so made them "converts." Like the aborigines of Western Australia, the Veddahs wear scarcely any clothing, and have no houses. In dry weather they sleep under the trees, and in the wet season creep into caves or crouch beneath the rocks in the mountains. This mode of life, I suppose, applies more or less to all savage nations, and no doubt prevailed in very ancient times in England.

In Great Namaqualand, also, a great and good work appeared to have been carried on at this period. The missionaries at first appeared to have suffered great hardship, food being so very scarce; but in a few years such was the success of the work that at a missionary meeting among the people the following contributions were made in gratitude to God, and to help forward the cause :—
3 cows, 10 oxen, 2 heifers, 4 calves, 147 sheep,

59 goats, and 1 bull. Such liberality needs no comment.

A feature in the Journals of the Rev. T. B. Freeman, describing his visits to Ashantee, was his special knowledge of botany. He appears to have been a close student of the flora of Western Africa. About this time there was a singular combination of names of missionaries on the Western Coast— Badger, Dove, Fox, and Swallow. This year a donation of £1000 was given, thus: "The late Rev. William Threlfall, missionary in South Africa, in accordance with his own request, and by the directions of his father, by his brother H. Threlfall, Esq., of Hollowforth." William Threlfall was foully murdered by some natives not long after entering on his missionary toil.

In connection with the Bible Society's gift of 5000 New Zealand New Testaments, before named, our missionary at Waima wrote: "Our people value the New Testament above everything, and they constantly read it with such attention that many of them find no difficulty in repeating whole Epistles from memory."

Many worthy owners and captains of sailing-ships are recorded as having given free passages to missionaries. These thoughtful acts of kindness and generosity were always greatly appreciated, and thankfully acknowledged by the Secretaries. To the late Mr. Lidgett and his worthy sons the Society was much indebted.

It was in this year that "Christmas Offerings" were suggested by Dr. Bunting, who thought that at least £3000 might be raised. The sum collected the first year was £4721. The venerable Doctor's wise suggestion has brought very many thousands of pounds into the Society's coffers.

1842

A terrible earthquake was reported this year from Hayti, when two-thirds of the town with 10,000 of its inhabitants were destroyed. A fire broke out after the earthquake, destroying the powder magazine, together with a considerable number of the miserable remnant of those who survived the earthquake itself. Great anxiety was felt for the Mission family there, but by God's mercy they were preserved. Poor Hayti, what she has suffered from disasters of almost every description, revolutions included!

Mr. Freeman gave an interesting account of the presentation by the Committee, of a carriage to the King of Ashantee. He told the King that it was sent by the Missionary Society as a token of their good feeling, and hoped he would use it, and that it would lead him to make good roads, etc. He added, that the carriage had been seen by the Queen of England. He replied: "The Queen of England is Queen of Queens of the white people, and I am King of Kings of the black people." It was an arduous task to get the carriage nearly two hundred miles through forests and jungle, and across rivers and deep ravines.

Large and special contributions now began to come in to meet the deficiencies of 1838, 1839, and 1840. Mr. Isaac Crowther, of Leeds, gave £1000, as did Mr. James Hargreaves, also of Leeds. The proceeds of the Sale of Ladies' Work at the Centenary Hall realised over £1600. The Centenary Fund voted £10,000, and the Dawsonian Fund realised over £1600.

A bitter feeling had subsisted for some time between the Boers and the English, and this led to open rebellion on the part of the Boers. They were led to expect that the King of Holland would support them in an attempt to establish themselves as an independent republic at Natal. Mr. Archbell, our missionary, wrote: "I will never conceal the atrocities which the Dutch farmers have committed since they went beyond the boundaries of the colony from the restraint of British law."

What may strike one as remarkable is a fact named in a speech at Exeter Hall, not far from this period of time, that it was never known that any missionary asked what his allowance would be, except once. In that case the young man was leaving a widowed mother behind.

1843

The Directors of the London Missionary Society issued a statement of the shameful aggression of the French on the island of Tahiti, resulting in the establishment of French sovereignty by force. It was a disgraceful transaction throughout. I believe it arose from the native authorities declining the services of the Catholic missionaries. This, at all events, was made the excuse. I name this as bearing somewhat on Mission work in the South Seas. It was, I believe, by an arrangement with the Directors that that Society took Tahiti under its pastoral care.

The year was ushered in by a terrible earthquake in Antigua and elsewhere, thirteen chapels and other Mission properties being destroyed. Then there was a dreadful fire at Kingston, in Jamaica, with a loss of from a quarter to half a million sterling. Mercifully, the Mission property escaped. A disaster like this would, as a matter of course, be somewhat of a hindrance to Mission work, at least to its finances.

The Rev. John Martin was appointed this year to the Gold Coast Mission, and laboured there for five years. On his return he married the daughter of Dr. Beecham. In course of time he became our "Super" at the Hackney Road Chapel. I greatly respected him. I mention these facts, adding that he is yet alive and resides near Stockport.

The Anniversary Meeting at Exeter Hall this year left an impression on my mind which led me, fifty years afterwards, to send the following communication to the *Methodist Recorder* :—

"Mr. Hayes (of the Allan Library) sends us his personal recollections of the Missionary Meeting at Exeter Hall fifty years ago (in 1843). He describes it as one of the most exciting meetings held there. The chair was occupied by Mr. J. P. Plumptre, in absence of Mr. (afterwards Sir) Emerson Tennent. Dr. Hannah was President that year, and spoke well. Peter Jacobs, a Chippewa Indian, pleaded for three-quarters of an hour for his people. He made a good impression, and excited much interest for the North American Indians. Dr. Leifchild was among the speakers, as was also Dr. Newton, who came out grandly, as he always did. In fact, none of the meetings at Exeter Hall seemed complete without him. The Rev. W. B. Boyce, just returned from South Africa, added much to the interest of the meeting. But the speaker who evoked the greatest applause was the Rev. Thomas Mortimer (a clergyman), son of Mrs. Mortimer, a personal friend of our venerable Founder. He wrought his audience up to a state of great enthusiasm. His reference to his mother and to the old preachers was most touching. It was a sight to see the speaker, a man of good presence, pointing to the clock, and calling out 'Time! time!' in reply to the calls to 'Go on! go on!' Some few of our readers may be able to recall this meeting to their memory."

The much revered R. Murray M'Cheyne, of

Dundee, preached one of the Society's sermons at the Anniversary.

1844

News of the deaths of the Rev. William Cross in 1842, and of Rev. David Cargill in 1843, was not received till the beginning of this year. What a contrast to the advantages we enjoy at the present day in the quick transmission of news!

The Hon. Fox Maule, afterwards Lord Panmure, Secretary for War, presided at the Annual Meeting. The next year the Marquis of Breadalbane took the chair. We used to get in those early times some of our best nobility for chairmen, but did not get such handsome donations from them as from our own people later on. At the Annual Meeting a donation of ten guineas was announced from the truly venerable Rev. Henry Moore, who died the previous Saturday.

In the latter part of the year the *Times* published a long letter, attacking Mr. Freeman and our Gold Coast Mission. Of course it was replied to; then the writer, "Omega," returned to the attack, and our long reply had to be paid for as an advertisement. It was considered by many to have been a shabby transaction on the part of the *Times*.

The Rev. William Moister told us of a marvellous escape he had from death by lightning while in an open boat accompanied by two boatmen, one of whom was struck dead in a moment. The other boatman was stunned, and Mr. Moister had all his work to do to navigate the boat to a place of safety. It was evident that the Almighty had more work for his honoured servant to do, which he nobly performed. He died in honoured old age, forty-five years afterwards.

Our learned "pundit," Robert Spence Hardy, wrote this year, in terms of sorrow and indignation, of the continued patronage by the Ceylon Government of the grossest idolatry, and how the conversion of the natives was hindered by it.

Later, we received news of the death of Josiah Tubon, King of the Friendly Islands, and of the succession of King George, a Methodist, who was long a nursing father to our Church there.

1845

Our truly valued Superintendent of Missions in Australia, the Rev. Walter Lawry, wrote early this year thus—

"It is more than twenty-two years ago since I landed at Auckland on my way to Tonga. Since then, what changes have taken place in this people! They were at war, and we saw many of their slaves brought into the bay, some of whom were killed and eaten on the beach. Now they crowd to market with their provisions, such as pigs, fowls, potatoes, etc., and abundance of fine fish; and, better still, they crowd to the house of prayer and read the word of God. Needless to say that missionary teaching has greatly helped to bring about such a change."

In the course of the year the Rev. W. B. Boyce went with his family, consisting of Mrs. Boyce and four young daughters, to Sydney, to take charge of the Australian Missions.

The British and Foreign Bible Society, with their accustomed liberality, made a grant of £1000 for expenses incurred during several years in translating the Bible into Kaffir.

1846

The missionary ship *Triton* not being well adapted for its work in the South Seas, though she had more than saved her original cost, the Committee caused a new ship to be built, larger and better adapted for the work, to be called the *John Wesley*. Messrs. White, of Ryde, the well-known shipbuilders, were the contractors. As had happened before, when the *Triton* was sent out by us, it was a busy time at the Mission House when the new ship was to start. Almost everything that it was thought would be useful was sent by friends of Missions for the use of the ship and the missionaries.

In due time the *John Wesley* left Southampton for its long voyage, under the command of Captain Buck, of the *Triton*, and carrying with it many prayers. The departure was a very interesting event. Dr. Beecham addressed the officers and crew in a very kind and affectionate manner, but the start was wisely delayed for a day or two beyond the time originally fixed, for a heavy gale came on in the night and continued all next day. The value of a vessel especially for the use of the Missions in the South Seas was forcibly shown in one instance, by a valuable missionary and his wife and children being at the point of starvation on the arrival of a vessel temporarily engaged to convey stores to them.   Mr. John Irving, a Bristol ship-owner, generously devoted much time in super-intending the building of the vessel and preparing it for its long voyage.

Towards the close of the year the Rev. Giffard Dorey embarked for British North America.   This veteran still lives, and is in active work as a Circuit Superintendent.   He is brother - in - law to Dr. Jenkins.

The Rev. John Walton, one of our ex-Presidents, was appointed this year to Ceylon.   He still survives, in honourable old age and rest.

1847

Early this year the very sudden death of the Rev. James Evans, of the Hudson's Bay Mission, took place at Kealby, just after he had ad-dressed the Missionary Meeting there.   He had accomplished a valuable work, before named, in regard to the Cree language.

A war, arising from a comparatively small cause, broke out between the English and the Kaffirs, causing a terrible loss of life to both sides. The enemy invaded the country at all points, and destroyed by fire every farmhouse and stack of grain, killed many of the inhabitants, and carried off thousands of cattle, sheep, and horses. Unfortunately, this was not the only war our Government had with the Kaffirs.

Bad news was received from Fiji, giving an account of the murder of the King of Rewa by the Bau heathen chiefs. The town of Rewa was utterly destroyed. Mr. Hunt adds: "But I must leave Rewa and its tale of woe for a brighter scene at Vewa. It is remarkable that, while Satan was triumphing at Rewa, the Lord was blessing us at Vewa with a most gracious revival."

Mr. Jaggar's letter, speaking of the value of the printing-press, says: "We are all engaged in preparing a correct version of the New Testament in Fiji. The people are all well supplied with catechisms." The Rev. R. B. Lyth writes that "God is with us in Fiji, and is pouring out His Spirit upon us."

The Rev. John Hunt, writing from Vewa, says of the papist missionaries who were forcing themselves on the native converts: "If they wish to convert men to Christianity, why not go to some of the places where there are no missionaries or native teachers? Why go and disturb the minds of people who are under the pastoral care of other missionaries?" A remarkable visitation of Divine grace in the Friendly Isles is recorded this year, hundreds being brought to accept Christ.

Our missionary at Canton de Vaud, in Switzerland, was peremptorily ordered by the Council of State to leave his work there within fifteen days, instead of the usual three months allowed. It was a piece of shameful intolerance, the more noticeable when it is remembered how the fathers of the Swiss fought and suffered to obtain liberty of conscience and freedom from oppression.

The Report of the Sierra Leone Theological Institution told of its success as an educational establishment. Six of the native young men had been appointed to various spheres of labour in connection with the Mission. Upon the preparation of an effective native ministry greatly depends, humanly speaking, the regeneration of the sons and daughters of Africa. The death of Governor Maclean of the Gold Coast was much regretted. He had been a good friend of the Mission, and was buried with his wife, the well-known poetess, L. E. L.

This year Dr. Alder, at the request of the Canada Committee of our Conference, was directed to proceed to Canada, with a view to the promotion of a union between the Western Canada Conference and the Societies under the care of our Missionary Society. It was an important mission, which the Doctor successfully carried through.

1848

A pleasing fact is recorded in a letter from the Rev. William Shaw, namely, that after the closing of the Butterworth Mission Station, arising from the Kaffir War, the chief, Krieli, earnestly desired that the Mission might be resumed, and said that he had proposed to make compensation for the damage the property had received. This proposal was in part carried out, but only in part, a loss of about £600 having to be made up in other ways. The letter written by Sir H. G. Smith, our representative at Cape Town, on the subject of the war, is worth quoting, it is so fatherly. "My son Krieli, twelve years ago I was your great friend, and, as I grieve to hear you have been led away by bad advice into a wicked war, so do I now rejoice to see you repentant to man, and I hope to God. . . . I pray you, therefore, to go to your missionary, and say he must make you worship God, as he and I, your father, and all good English people do; then would God Almighty bless you, your cattle would increase, your fields be covered with houses and cultivation; then would you bless the English, through that great God Almighty who brought them among your people. Do this, my son, and you will live to thank your father, and to hope for eternal life and happiness hereafter."

Mr. Lawry's long letters, published in the *Notices*

late this year, gave details of Fijian cannibalism too horrible to quote, though it was thought at the time that they should not be suppressed. In many cases cannibalism did not take place from want of food, but from sheer love of human flesh and blood. It was affirmed that within the four years preceding fully one thousand people had been killed within twenty miles of Vewa, and that it was within compass to say that of those slain five hundred had been eaten. The leaven of Christianity, however, was slowly but surely working among these savage islanders, and, as we have before noticed, it brought in a few years a most marvellous change.

The death of Dr. John Hunter, of Islington, one of the old-fashioned courtly surgeons of former days, was announced. He kindly doctored me once or twice. Dr. Lindoe, a lover of mankind, also passed away this year.

1849

More of the Journals of the Rev. Walter Lawry's visits, as General Superintendent, to the South Seas were issued in the early part of this year. Looking through them recently, I was greatly impressed with their value. The information they contain is so varied and full of interest that they may fairly be placed among our missionary classics. The Secretaries did well to issue them to the public in book form.

The account of the Rev. William Shaw's tour of inspection through the Missions embraced in the Natal and Kaffraria Districts, also well repaid careful reading. Mr. Shaw was a grand old missionary, and I well remember his stately and dignified manner. We often afterwards saw him at the Mission House, where he was a welcome visitor.

The State persecution in the Canton de Vaud, spoken of recently, appeared to increase in intensity, and prayer to the Almighty was earnestly urged by the Committee on behalf of the sufferers. It was an instance of the malignant hostility of the infidel Antichrist against vital Christianity— an evil influence which is always worst when it is helped by civil power and secular authority.

In connection with the Missionary Anniversary, the Rev. John Jordan, Vicar of Enstone, in Oxfordshire, had engaged to preach on behalf of our Society's Missions at the Episcopal Chapel in Gray's Inn Lane, kindly lent by the Rev. Thomas Mortimer, but at the last moment the Bishop of London forbade it. Lord Ashley, afterwards Earl of Shaftesbury, wrote that he was grieved at the prohibition. Mr. Mortimer, too, expressed his regret at the Bishop's action. Mr. Jordan spoke at the Annual Meeting, regretting what the Bishop had done. Dr. Norman Macleod was one of the speakers.

The lamented death of the Rev. John Hunt was

reported in the April *Notices*. For me to say a word in praise of this noble missionary would be an impertinence. What a work he did in his short ten years of missionary life ! " His works do follow him." Mr. Lawry, on one of his voyages, speaking of Mr. Hunt, said : " Mr. Hunt preached. He poured forth thought upon thought, so just, so weighty, so original, so luminous, that I sat upon the quarter - deck looking at this wonderful man with amazement and admiration. The scene was altogether lovely, — the setting sun, the cloud-capped mountains, the placid ocean, the listening crew, the native teachers, and the intelligent preacher from whom were coming forth ' rivers of living water.' "

News of a severe earthquake in the southern part of New Zealand came to hand, occasioning a heavy loss of Mission property, as well as much precuniary loss and suffering to the people. Our missionary at Swan River, among the aboriginal natives, wrote hopefully of his work. The arrival of the Rev. Geo. Parsonson and his wife at Algoa Bay eighty - five days after leaving Gravesend is noteworthy. To us this seems a long voyage. I was much attached to Mr. and Mrs. Parsonson ; and when their son, many years afterwards reader at the Conference Office, knew that I was so very friendly with his parents, he was very pleased, and I seemed to live over again my early friendship.

The Rev. Peter Percival, of Jaffna, who had been

employed at the request of the Bible Society, reported the translation of the entire Bible into Tamil, for which the Committee heartily congratulated him.

1850

The Government Mission to Ashantee was reported in part in the January *Notices*, and is very interesting reading. The departure of the Rev. T. T. N. Hull and Mrs. Hull for Adelaide, Australia, was also announced. This veteran, who entered the ministry in 1826, still lives, and is the oldest Wesleyan minister in the Connexion. He resides in Ireland. Mr. John Chubb generously presented an iron tomb to be placed over the grave of the late Rev. John Hunt. The Waldenses of Piedmont were visited by the Rev. M. Gallienne. He gives an interesting account of his visit. The sufferings of these worthy people in defence of liberty of conscience is a matter of history. The Society's income was reported to be £7500 in advance of the preceding year.

The Annual Meeting at Exeter Hall was a somewhat tumultuous one. When the resolution was moved for the adoption of the Report, an attempt was made by one of the audience to move an amendment, but Mr. Fox Maule (afterwards Lord Panmure), who presided, refused to accept it, and, on finding the meeting was against him, the would-be mover subsided into silence.

The *John Wesley* ship this year had a narrow escape from being captured by a piratical band, on her way from Sydney to New Zealand. We were gladdened by news of the conversion of Tungi, a heathen Tongan chief, and more than one hundred of his people; the remaining stronghold of heathenism being thus subjected to Christ.

CHAPTER VI

1851

AT the Annual Missionary Meeting this year, Mr. Lawry, then at home, made a deeply interesting speech; in fact, for what he said, it might be called the speech of the day. Among other good things he said, was that he would give a family contribution of £500 to the Society's funds. This generosity showed his love for the work in which he had been engaged for many years. He went to New South Wales in 1817, to the Friendly Islands in 1820, and succeeded Mr. Waterhouse as General Superintendent. He died in 1859. His was a face one could not help loving, so placid and kind. -He left a good memory behind him.

The *John Wesley* brought to England a shipload of articles—shells, coral, clubs, spears, and other weapons, given by the native converts. This sale was a very successful one, both in attendance and financially. A few of the items are yet in my possession. The cowrie shells were remarkably fine specimens.

Remarkable effects of prayer in averting war in Fiji were recorded this year. While the Christian natives were praying, the opposing warriors were seized with fear. "The longer we stayed, the more faint-hearted we grew," they said.

Owing to the wars among the tribes of South Africa, and the consequent destruction of some of the Mission stations, the missionaries were having a very bad time there. "The people were swept away, and thousands of cattle stolen. . . . But what African missionary is without trials?" asks our agent.

A form of Bequest to the Society's funds was this year settled upon by the Committee, after the opinion of counsel had been obtained upon the subject. The learned counsel consulted was Mr. Richard Matthews, of the Temple, who had at various times rendered good service by his advice.

At the Annual Meeting, Dr. Duff, the grand Indian missionary, made a noble speech, which elicited loud and prolonged cheers. The Rev. R. D. Griffith also pleaded earnestly for two hundred millions of our fellow-subjects in India.

Later on in the year, Mr. Lawry in his Journals gives a letter from King George to him, part of which is too good to withhold. "O Mr. Lawry, the good which I have received through the Christian religion is, that I know the truth of the gospel, and its preciousness and value to my soul. I have received the forgiveness of my sins, and am justified by the blood of Christ. God has adopted me as His son, and made my soul anew.   I have a hope beyond death, because of Christ.   The benefits of this religion to Tonga are that it has brought peace to our land.   Its settled and happy condition we all attribute to religion's influence.   O that the Lord would at once grant that long may be your life, Mr. Lawry."   Later on, Mr. Lawry writes: "There is not much idle bread eaten in Fiji. Mr. Lyth has the sick to attend, beside his Mission affairs; Mrs. Lyth has her family and the barter going on; Mr. Malvern has his native school and his Mission work; Mrs. Malvern has the children of the two families every alternate week, and also her family engagements.   There is no time to be dull in the Mission work."

What shall I say of the Great Exhibition this year?   Though it had no special bearing on our Missions, the greatness of the event cannot be passed by.   Among the treasures shown in the famous "Palace of Glass" was a good collection of missionary exhibits.   I believe our Society took part in this.   I visited the Great Exhibition twice or thrice, but cannot describe its effect upon me. Someone has said that it was worth being born to have seen it.   London was in a state of great excitement over it.   "Everybody" went to see it.

1852

Our native agent in Ashantee, Ossu Ansah, was of the royal family of Ashantee, and was educated in England. After his return the gospel came to his heart with power, and he willingly devoted himself to the work of the Mission. After a time he was judged capable of conducting the Mission in the capital of his native kingdom.

The munificent legacy of £10,000, bequeathed by the late Mr. Thomas Marriott, was announced early this year.

China now appears for the first time in the Minutes. Two years before, Mr. Piercy went out at his own expense, and his communications were so satisfactory and pleasing that he was received as one of the Society's missionaries. He laboured there for thirty-two years, then in 1883 took charge of the work among Chinese sailors in London, and last year (1901) he visited his old scenes of labour in China at his own expense. He is a man whom I greatly respect, as well for his friendliness as for his work's sake. The Rev. Josiah Cox was this year set apart for work in the "Celestial Empire." I have a pleasing recollection of Mr. Cox before his departure. He spent twenty-four years there, and is now resting from Mission work, though not leading an idle life, in Jersey. I am pleased to include him as one of my old friends.

At a meeting of the Royal Geographical Society in London, high testimony was borne to the value of the Society's work in the Training Institution at Tonga. The Hon. Captain Keppel's examination of the pupils, on the maps, etc., was very satisfactory.

It was pleasing to find that our Government had undertaken a nautical survey of Fiji, whose coral reefs and dangerous shores have so often imperilled our missionary ship and missionaries in their frequent voyages among the islands. Captain Denham, the commander of the expedition, favoured the Missionary Secretaries with repeated interviews on board his ship, while lying at Woolwich, and received from them copies of the Fijian Grammar recently published by our missionary Hazlewood. Captain Denham also spoke of the important help he had obtained from the influence of our missionary at Badagry, the Rev. John Martin, when surveying that part of the West African coast.

Governor Macdonnell of the Gambia called at the Mission House and told of the value of Mrs. Badger's labours there. He also spoke of the efforts of the Rev. Henry Badger during the past year as most zealous. It is pleasing to have such testimonies borne by those high in office to the value of our agents.

The retirement of Dr. Bunting from active service at the Mission House was characterised by a most gratifying communication from our sister Church in the United States, equally honourable to the senders as to the recipients of it.

1853

War broke out early this year in Tonga, some of the heathen chiefs refusing obedience to the laws, and erecting forts in defiance. King George exercised great forbearance, declining to storm the forts, as they sheltered the Romish priests, who were said to have encouraged the chiefs in their rebellion. One of our missionaries was fired at, and some of the best men of Tonga were slain or wounded. The missionaries wisely refrained from countenancing the war in any way.

A remarkable revival was reported from Sierra Leone, and among the natives there was a general abandonment of their idol gods. It was cheering to hear that many of the negro wizards were among those who gave up their false gods.

This year Dr. Punshon (then Mr.) was for the first time. among the missionary preachers and speakers at the Anniversary. I shall have to speak of this great orator later on. A few words of his speech at Exeter Hall are worth repeating. " If the world is to be converted, it must be by the simple preaching of the gospel. Statesmanship, we find, has gathered up its wisdom for the trial, and has gathered it up in vain. Colonisation adventured on the task of reclaiming the savage, and it has failed. Education, though it can acquaint a man with all knowledge, can never teach him repentance towards God, or distil from his obdurate heart one solitary motion of godly sorrow."

The rush to the gold-fields in Australia at this time was so immense that it became necessary to open an Emigrants' Home for Wesleyan emigrants. Much hardship was experienced for want of accommodation for the crowds arriving. The Home did good service for a long time, and was an honour to those who suggested it.

The death of the venerable Benjamin Clough, uncle to Dr. Punshon, took place in April, after a forty years' ministry. He was one of those who embarked with Dr. Coke on his last voyage in 1813. He laboured in Ceylon for twenty-five years. His genial face and kindly manner were very pleasant.

The insurrection in China engaged the earnest attention of the Committee this year. At first the rebellion rolled on in full tide, but eventually it was suppressed, largely by the help of General Gordon, better known after that as " Chinese Gordon." The Secretaries issued in the October *Notices* a most valuable paper on the rebellion. The missionaries acknowledged there was cause for both fear and hope. This was certain, that China was more open to missionary work than ever. A singular feature of the rebellion was that the leader of it issued the Book of Genesis at his own expense at the time. In the meantime the Bible Society took measures for the circulation of one million copies of the Chinese New Testament.

This year the Commander of H.M.S. *Fire-Fly* called at the Mission House, and bore gratifying testimony of the value of the Society's work on the Gold Coast.

1854

The Australian Colonies soon began to feel their responsibility in providing increased means of grace for the crowds of emigrants reaching their shores, and this they did with no niggardly hand. The gold discoveries had filled the land with people from all parts, many of whom were Methodists. Our missionary at Sydney pleasingly writes that he " considers the piety of the members has suffered no abatement by the influx of temporal prosperity."

The Committee had a long and interesting interview with the Rev. Dr. Taylor, the eminent Chinese missionary. He was the only missionary who had been in personal communication with the insurgents.

On April 3rd the Rev. Robert Young safely returned, after successfully accomplishing the great objects of his mission. He visited the Australian Colonies, Van Diemen's Land, New Zealand, the Friendly and the Fiji Islands, calling at Ceylon and

Gibraltar. I remember how warmly he was welcomed at the Mission House.

Mr. Young spoke grandly at the Exeter Hall Meeting, and remarked that he was struck with the reverence paid to the Lord's Day in the Friendly Islands. He said he never saw the Sabbath so hallowed in any part of the world. He further told us of his landing at Bau, " doubtless the deepest hell upon earth." " On nearing the shore a native came out, and in the politest manner landed me out of the boat. I took off my hat and made him a low bow, on which Mr. Calvert smiled, and said, ' You little know who you are bowing to: that man is the fiercest cannibal in the place.' I was shown six ovens, in which eighteen human victims had recently been cooked." Mr. Young issued a handsome volume describing his *Visit to the Southern World.*

The Rev. Henry Badger, having received £500 for his duties as chaplain at St. Mary's, Gambia, generously presented it as a gift to the Society.

An interesting account was given in the September *Quarterly Papers* of Joel Bulu, our native missionary at Lakemba. His letter to the Committee was characteristic. " My love to you is very great, and I earnestly wish it was an easy thing for me to go and meet with you, that these eyes might look upon your countenances, and that these two hands of mine might take hold of yours and shake them. Thanks, thanks, thanks for your love, which was manifested in your sending us missionaries to preach Jesus to us."

An interesting account of Elijah Varani was given in the September *Quarterly Papers.* "The name of Varani is familiar to those who are acquainted with the history of the Mission in Fiji. Notorious for deeds of treachery and blood while a heathen, he became, on embracing the Christian religion, remarkable for the consistency of his deportment, and the zeal with which he preached the faith which he once destroyed. His conversion took place in 1845, and it was an event for which the missionaries had long prayed."

1855

Particulars of the conversion from heathenism of the great Fijian King Thakombau was given in the January *Notices.* It was added · "Many friends of this Mission will rejoice with the missionaries who are spared to see this signal fruit of their long toil." Mr. Calvert, writing of the completion of the New Testament into Fijian by the Bible Society, says that at least 5000 copies will be required; already 4000 persons can read the Scriptures, and the number is daily increasing. He tells, however, of the dark side of the picture, and speaks of sons strangling their mothers to accompany their dead husbands into the next world; of parents burying their infants alive in the houses they were living in; of fathers killing their daughters, and of others strangling their sick brothers. Further details of these horrors cannot be given, they are too dreadful. One widow insisted on being put to death, and the missionary had to drag her away by main force; eventually he got her to a Christian town. One is the more astonished at the change which in time took place in such people; nothing but the power of God could have effected it.

Dr. Beecham left in May on a mission of great importance to British North America, which he successfully accomplished. Full particulars were given in the November and December *Notices*.

The Kaffir chief Kama, of whom we read in later years, was one of three brothers, chiefs of one of the largest native tribes, and was baptized by the Rev. William Shaw. "He is now an eminent Christian and preacher of the gospel." The September *Quarterly Papers* give a most interesting account of the Mission to Kama's tribe. His portrait represents him, not in his "war paint," but as a preacher in English clothing.

1856

A long letter from Dr. Hervey, Professor of Botany, while on a scientific visit to the Fiji and Friendly Islands, addressed to his friend, Mr. Ward, F.R.S., is too good to be wholly passed by; but one small extract must suffice. "Not long ago a case occurred in Fiji, when a wretch ordered his wife to heat the oven, and when she had done so she asked, 'Where is the food?' 'You are the food,' was the savage's reply, as he instantly clubbed her, and then cooked her for himself and party. The captain of our vessel told me that the last time he was in Fiji, in 1847, he saw a hundred human bodies laid out at one time for cooking at a great feast. Picture to yourself a people like this, numbering perhaps 200,000 souls ; then see a small band of missionaries with their wives and families sitting down among them, with their lives in their hands (literally a living sacrifice, holy and acceptable to God), and thus living on without human protection for years and years, seeing scarcely any fruit of their labours, till their heads are growing grey, or till some of their number have been laid in a Fijian grave,—and then behold this same people, after twenty years' labours, appealing by its 10,000 converts to the sympathies of a Christian world : contrast these pictures, and I think you will join me in praying that God may prosper this great work, and that speedily." The worthy Professor, in a second letter to his friend, writes : " If you wish to know what the Wesleyans are doing at Fiji, get the Rev. Robert Young's *Southern - World*, recently published. It gives a true picture of the state of society two years ago. . . . Heathenism is fast breaking up, and thousands more than can be supplied with teachers are anxious to *lotu*. They now count the attendants on public worship at

30,000, being more than treble what they were last year." Such unsought testimony from an independent witness is very valuable.

The death of the Rev. David Hazlewood, of the Fiji Mission, was reported. He died at the early age of thirty-six, but he had crowded much good work into his short life, having translated the Old Testament into Fijian and written a Fijian Grammar. Praise God for such a life!

Dr. Punshon again spoke at this year's Annual Meeting, and in his speech said: " I was reading the other day, as a sort of refresher before I came to this meeting, an article by Sydney Smith, written in the *Edinburgh Review*, upon Indian Missions. In that article the reverend lampooner insinuates that there is some little affinity between evangelism and disloyalty; affects great alarm for our Indian Empire; prophesies the utter hopelessness of India's conversion by 'Sectaries,' as he calls them; and asks, ' Why should we send out our little detachments of maniacs to give distorted views of Christianity to the finest provinces of the world?' "

The presentation of a fine bust of the late Dr. Newton was made this year by Mr. Walton, proprietor of the famous Carrara marble works in Italy, for deposit in the Centenary Hall. It was a beautiful work of art.

1857

The territory in which the Hudson's Bay Company carry on their trade is very great, and is supposed to extend to more than 4,000,000 square miles. It is, in short, one-third larger than Europe. The Company was formed in London in 1669, under the direction of Prince Rupert, for the purpose of prosecuting the fur trade. As before stated, good work has been done by our missionaries, greatly helped and encouraged by the Directors of the Company. At this date (1857) there were five of our missionaries and five stations. Our agents spoke of the prosperity of their efforts, beyond their most sanguine expectations.

The lamented death of our deputation to Western Africa, the Rev. Daniel West, took place early this year. He had concluded his mission, and was about to return, but was seized with illness on board the *Niger*. He was taken on shore, and died at St. Mary's, Gambia. To the account of Mr. West's death was added: " It is peculiarly afflictive that he should have been taken from us at this juncture of his services to the Church of Christ. This mysterious event will be cleared up in the light of eternity."

The British and the Chinese had again fallen out, and war with its horrors was asserting itself. In their foolish rage the Chinese destroyed all British property in Canton, and drove out all its English inhabitants. For a time the Mission was suspended.

Of course the Chinese had afterwards to pay a heavy bill. Alas, poor China!

At the Exeter Hall Meeting Mr. Calvert spoke long and forcibly. He told us of an interview he had with a cannibal chief who had just strangled his mother and two of his wives. He said: " I went to the King's house, and found him asleep. On awaking he asked me what I wanted. I told him that I came to plead with him that the wives of a chief who had just died might not be strangled. He replied, ' I cannot give it up, it is our custom.' On my leaving him he was heard to say, ' What a marvellous thing it is ! These missionaries do not care how far they go, or what trouble they take to save our lives, whilst we do not care what we do that we may destroy one another.' In another interview the chief said, ' I hate your Christianity.' I said, ' I knew that before I left England. Though you hate us, what are you going to do with it ? Will you stop it ? ' ' No,' said he, ' I cannot do that. I know we shall all become Christians.' This chief has become a Christian ; and not only he, but 50,000 people have followed his example."

This was the year when the Sepoy rebellion broke out among the Bengal native troops. It would require the pen of a " ready writer " to describe the horrors of that time, the sufferings of the European families, the slaughter of the native converts, and other atrocities. Suffice it to say that in the end England's power subdued the rebellion, and, after it had been suppressed, it was decided that there should be fewer native and more English troops than before.   The real object of the conspiracy was the destruction of British power in India, and the re-establishment of Mohammedan rule.   Many of the Hindu sepoys were deluded into joining the Mutiny, by the pretext that their religion was in danger.   To our disgrace be it known that Mohammedanism and Hinduism have not been merely tolerated, they have been rewarded and pampered, whilst Christianity has been frowned upon.

The Rev. J. S. Banks, writing from Bangalore, says; " We cannot but look on these calamities as God's righteous punishment for the marked disregard of Christianity by our rulers.   The Bible is a forbidden book in every Government school, college, and university. . .   It is a contradiction that we cannot understand, and would fain see removed, that a Christian Government should take the utmost pains to preserve its millions of subjects in all their heathen darkness, and exclude that truth which alone truly reveals the security of Government and the welfare of the people. . . . Our Indian rulers give tens of thousands annually to support Mohammedanism and Hinduism, to support feasts and temples and idols and priests, . . . whilst they give not one penny, that I am aware of, directly for the conversion of the natives to Christianity."

I love the name of Thomas Champness.   I knew

him before he went to West Africa this year, where he spent seven years for the Master. How he has laboured since then is well known to all Methodism, and his *Joyful News* Mission is still a power for good.

1858

Early this year a large meeting was held at Exeter Hall, presided over by the Earl of Shaftesbury. It was one of the most representative meetings ever held there, and was convened to draw the most earnest attention of the Government to its State aid of idolatry, especially by discontinning all grants for the maintenance of heathen temples and idol worship, and ceasing to administer endowments for their support; by preventing all acts of cruelty, and all obscene exhibitions connected with idolatrous rites; and by entirely withholding its sanction to social evils connected with the system of caste. The noble chairman spoke out grandly on the occasion.

The death of the Rev. Charles Cook took place in February. He was President of the French Conference at the time of his death, and he had been engaged in the French work for many years. He was a man highly respected and beloved. Christians of all denominations held him in high esteem. He was a faithful servant to his Master for forty-two years. I have a vivid recollection of the venerable man.

A remarkable instance of a missionary's love for the scenes of his early labours was shown by the offer of the Rev. Samuel Brown to return to Sierra Leone, after an absence of forty years. He went there in 1816, and again in 1858.

Next to John Wesley, I suppose no man had influenced Methodism more than Dr. Bunting, who died this year full of years and honours. It would be superfluous for me to say anything of this great man. His "Life," written by his son, Mr. T. P. Bunting, and the Rev. G. S. Rowe, shows the greatness of the man. I held him in the deepest respect, and my veneration was mingled with much love for him.

A remarkable letter which had been received from the Rev. E. E. Jenkins appeared in the August *Notices*, and excited intense interest. It told of a young Indian convert desiring baptism, of the efforts of his parents to prevent it, and of the fierce attack on Mr. Jenkins and Mr. Cockill by an infuriated mob. They had to run for their lives, and barely escaped, for the savage mob swarmed through the Mission house, bent upon their destruction. The damage done was considerable. By their action, the native police were evidently in concert with the rioters. Mr. Jenkins in a later letter said : " Last Sunday morning Viziarangum was baptized. The behaviour and answers of the young convert were very satisfactory. A large number of heathen natives were present, and profound quiet and attention rested upon all. After the baptism, the Rev. John Walton preached an able and impressive sermon.

The Bible Society kindly placed this year at the Committee's disposal in the Mysore 5000 copies of each of the four Gospels in the Canarese language, being 20,000 volumes for so many families.

1859

This year began with an account of some very high-handed proceedings on the part of the French in the Friendly Islands, arising from the unwillingness of the King to receive the Catholic priests. The action of the French in the Friendly Islands was very much like that which occurred some years before in Tahiti.

A good friend of the Society gave £1000 in memory of the late Joseph Carne, Esq., of Penzance. He was for many years our District Missionary Treasurer, and I had much correspondence with him in his official capacity.

A Ladies' Committee was formed this year for the "-Amelioration of the Condition of Women in Heathen Countries, and for Female Education." Mrs. Hoole was the life and soul of the movement, and it grew into great proportions. Mrs. Wiseman, a lady full of good works, is now the praiseworthy secretary.

The death of the Rev. E. J. Hardey at a village on the banks of the river Cauvery was reported.

He was engaged in the work of Bible distribution, and was seized with cholera, which in one short day's illness ended a truly valuable life, and one full of great promise. "He was buried far from any Christian graves, among the heathen. Even they, in committing him to his last rest, said, 'A good man should be laid in good ground.' But a converted Brahmin kneeled by the grave, and offered a funeral prayer to the God of life and the Author of resurrection from the dead."

Another revolution, resulting in the downfall of a tyrannical king and the establishment of a republic, was reported from Hayti by our worthy missionary, Mark B. Bird. If ever a missionary was "cradled in a storm," it was he. What with revolutions, hurricanes, disastrous fires, etc., he had his full share of trouble. He wrote: "Thus has ended the reign of a dark night of ignorance, injustice, and oppression, during which some of the faithful servants of the Most High have suffered bonds and imprisonments, and many an honest man has wept and groaned and died." Mr. Bird, a man of small stature, was every inch a missionary.

The remarkable revival of religion in Ireland, which stirred all Christendom and puzzled the secular press, can only be referred to in a few lines. Our missionary at Coleraine wrote: "I preached here seven times outside, and three inside, doors. No pen can describe the work that is going on in this Circuit. Some of the meetings were of

6

an extraordinary character, so many struck down and crying for mercy, shouting for joy, with the clapping of their hands; others singing praises, etc., that the scene could hardly be conceived by those who had not seen it." This experience was that of many places where the revival broke out. England and Ireland largely shared in the blessing.

A legacy of £10,000, less duty, by Mr. Thomas Pooll, of Road, Somerset, was reported, the second of a similar amount, the first being that of Mr. Thomas Marriott.

1860

An interesting account is given in the January *Notices* of a deputation of several members of the Missionary Committee having waited on Sir George Grey to present a memorial expressive of the sense they entertained of the many benefits he had been instrumental in conferring on the aboriginal inhabitants and the colonists of Southern Africa and New Zealand. The members of the deputation were introduced individually to Sir George by the Rev. William Shaw, who had been personally acquainted with His Excellency in South Africa and since his return to this country. Sir George recognised the Rev. W. B. Boyce as the author of the Kaffir Grammar, and as having visited New Zealand during his government of that colony. He added that he had consulted the Rev. William Shaw, whose suggestions were so distinguished by practical wisdom, connected with a thorough knowledge of the native character, that he found them of the utmost value to himself and his government, and all these suggestions had been successfully carried into effect. He spoke in the highest terms of the Christian natives of New Zealand and South Africa.

From Boulogne news was received of a very gratifying character. "We have had a glorious work here. The chapel nearly full every day. Such a time Boulogne never witnessed before. We had no voice. It ' was the speechless awe that dares not move, and all the silent heaven of love.' "

Pity poor Fiji! What a watchword was this in former days! " When first this cry was raised, it awoke a deep and practical sympathy in the heart of our Church. The tale of degradation and death was so terrible that it made every ear tingle and all Christian hearts pray. Now we ask the Christian to ' turn aside and see this great sight.' Nearly one-third of this Aceldama is reclaimed from heathen darkness and deeds of violence. There the fires of the destroyer are extinguished, the ovens are filled up, heathen temples are overthrown or converted into Christian schools. . . . 60,000 Fijians have divorced the barbarities, the obscenities, and pollutions of heathenism."

Dr. Punshon seemed now by public consent and expectation to have succeeded Dr. Newton at

Exeter Hall. His speeches were grand deliveries, and were always listened to with intensity. How we used to hang upon his lips! The Rev. William Wilson, better known as " Fiji Wilson," at home at that time, pleaded earnestly for his Mission, where there was yet much to be done. His speech occupied ten columns of the *Notices.* His Scottish accent added a charm to his impassioned eloquence.

Later in the year is given a Report of Mr. Arthur's visit to Bradford to examine the working of the Juvenile Missionary Association system, introduced by Mr. Blake, of Harrow. I remember how Mr. Blake " pegged away " with his scheme till it was gradually adopted in most or very many Circuits. The results of the " Blake System " have exceeded the most sanguine expectation.

CHAPTER VII

A MISSIONARY RETROSPECT, 1861–1871

1861

HER Majesty's Government found it necessary to administer a rebuke and warning to the King of Dahomey, on account of his excessive cruelty, shown in the recent "customs," and of his threats to the partially Christian city of Abbeokuta. The missionary wrote: "Light and darkness are now in conflict." The accounts sent by Mr. Bernasko are horrible in the extreme. Two thousand victims were sacrificed. The missionary had to read the letter from our authorities to the King, and he added: "He seems quite frightened." The threat was to destroy his towns on the sea-coast. Surely the Almighty has given England her great power for the purpose of preventing such atrocities.

Mr. J. Robinson Kay, of Bury, a man full of good deeds, sent to the Committee £1000, particularly with respect to China, etc. "A Wesleyan lady," by Mr. Heald, sent a similar amount with the same words, so I suppose Mr. and Mrs. Kay were the donors. All honour to their memory!

Dr. Gervase Smith was a welcome speaker at Exeter Hall. This year he spoke very effectively, and quoted a poem beautifully appropriate. I cannot help giving the first verse—

We plead for those lands, where a beautiful light
Is slow stealing over the hill-top and vale;
Where broad is the field and the harvest is white,
But the reapers are haggard and pale.

The poem goes on, speaking of the missionary and his young wife, " all wasted and worn with their wearisome toil." I have seen many painful sights of returned missionaries and wives, completely broken down with climate and toil, in some cases coming home only to die, and they have filled me with sorrow. I will give another quotation from Dr. Smith, too eloquent to withhold. Speaking of the appropriateness, the complete fitness of the gospel for every nationality: " What did the missionaries preach to the Greenlanders? The gospel! What did Dr. Coke preach to the Negro? The gospel! What is Dr. Duff preaching to the literati of Calcutta? The gospel! What is Dr. Jenkins preaching in Madras? The gospel! What does Wilson preach in Fiji? The gospel! And Piercy in China? Still the gospel! Oh, sir, I rejoice to think that the prophecy is now approaching its fulfilment: 'There is no speech nor language where their voice is not heard. Their line is gone through all the earth, and their words to the ends of the world.'" There was a *bonhomie* in Dr. Smith which drew people to him. One winter evening I heard him lecture at Exeter Hall, and during the delivery of the lecture it rained heavily and then froze. How the crowded audience got home I don't know, as all horse traffic was stopped, but I remember that I crept along the gutters to get a foothold in my three-mile walk.

The death of Mr. Thomas Farmer, the Society's munificent Treasurer, took place a few days after the Exeter Hall Meeting. Illness prevented his attendance. He sent a cheque for £500 for the China Mission. In Mr. Farmer the Missionary Society lost one of its best friends, if not its very best friend. He was wise in counsel, a man of business habits, and his liberality knew no bounds. It is not for me to speak in his praise. I think his " Life " should have been written ; we have lost by the omission. In all seasons his beautiful " buttonhole " was noticeable.

The importance of a new chapel in Paris now engaged the earnest attention of the Missionary Committee. A room in the Rue Royale had been rented for a long time, and it could not long be retained. The site of the present handsome building being in the hands of a Protestant gentleman, it was secured to us on favourable terms. A Parisian architect of high character gave his services gratuitously. In such a commanding spot it necessarily cost a large amount. In a visit to Paris some years ago I was pleased to see what a beautiful building it was. The chapel is on an upper floor, and is a very fine one.

1862

The printing - press has been of inestimable value to our Mission work, and its operations may well be regarded with interest. Eight presses at this period were maintained by the Society. That at Colombo reports that every month 10,000 copies of tracts, periodicals, and portions of Holy Scripture are issued and distributed among the native Singhalese. At Bangalore the printing of a quarto edition of the New Testament in the Canarese language has been completed, and the whole Bible is now for the first time available in this language in one volume. 22,000 of St. John's Gospel, 17,000 of the Acts, 5000 of the Epistles, 30,000 Canarese tracts, averaging 30 pages each, 15,000 schoolbooks, etc., have been printed. At Mount Coke, in Kaffraria, the year's work was as follows:—3000 first Kaffir spelling-books, 2000 second ditto, 2000 prayer - books, 500 Luther's catechisms, 500 Luther's hymn-books, 1000 Proverbs, and many more, all in Kaffir. At Thaba 'Nchu, in the Bechuana country, upwards of 300,000 pages have been printed. Great success has attended the work of the other presses.

Dr. George Smith, of Camborne, presided this year at the Exeter Hall Meeting. He was a man of whom Methodism might well be proud. Though a manufacturer, he found time to write a number of most valuable works. The *History of Wesleyan Methodism*, in three thick octavo volumes, is a monument of his labour. At his request, I had the pleasure of searching through a set of the *Imperial Magazine* for items which might be of use to him in that work.

The Rev. Josiah Cox told us of visits he made to the "Shield King," one of the leaders of the Ta-ping rebellion, whom he knew in former days. Mr. Cox wrote: "My visit enabled me to offer a few words of earnest counsel to him, and expressed the solicitude with which the Ta-pings are watched in England." He had a three hours' interview with him. It was a long and most interesting communication.

An account of the visit of Dr. Jenkins and the Rev. G. Fryar up the Godavery River was published in the October *Notices*. It occupied nearly eight pages, and was a valuable contribution to our missionary literature.

The death of the Rev. Horatio Pearse took place at D'Urban, Natal, amidst the regrets of the whole population, by whom he was universally respected and beloved. Also that of the Rev. John Ayliff, at Fauresmith, in the Orange Free State. One of his last sayings was, "Oh, glorious work! If I had ten thousand lives, I would devote them all to Mission work." Appropriate from such a missionary as he was.

Our General Superintendent at Cape Coast, the Rev. W. West, was told by our agent at Dahomey that the barbarian who ruled that country was anxious to have a visit from him (Mr. West), and adds: " My own opinion is that the King would regard me as a most eligible hostage for the safety of Whydah from the threats of our commander on the coast." The November *Notices* give an account of a forced visit to Dahomey by a Dutch merchant. The details are sickening, and one part only can be quoted, namely, that in the market-place he saw the body of the Church Missionary Agent (a Sierra Leone man) at Ishagga, captured with many more when the place was taken by the King, crucified against a large tree——one nail through the forehead, one through the heart, and one through each hand and foot.

1863

In preparation for the approaching Jubilee of the Missionary Society, an account of the Society's operations during that period was given in the *Notices*. Fifty years ago Methodism in British North America had its centres in Newfoundland, in Prince Edward Island, and in seven Circuits in Nova Scotia and New Brunswick. Now it had a Conference of its own, and reports 15,389 members, 1448 on trial, and 86 ministers, with 40 probationers and 13 supernumeraries. The Canada Conference had 50,311 members, 4064 on trial, 314 ministers, 111 probationers, and 61 supernumeraries, while fifty years ago there was no announcement of British Methodism throughout the whole region now occupied by the Canada Conference. Fifty years ago no mention was made of Methodism in Australia or Van Diemen's Land, much less of New Zealand and the Friendly and Fiji Islands. Fifty years ago our nearest approach to France was through the French prisoners at Dartmoor and in the Medway. Fifty years ago a solitary station at Sierra Leone represented the West Coast.

An earnest appeal for New Guinea was made by Mr. Arthington, of Leeds, backed by a liberal offer of help. He wrote: "It is high time that New Guinea was entered by missionaries. It is an island of 260,000 square miles." This Mission is now worked by one of the Australian Conferences. Belize, in Central America, experienced the calamity of having had half the town destroyed by fire. Our chapel, schoolhouse, etc., were destroyed.

Now we come to the Missionary Jubilee, which the Committee earnestly urged should be a successful one. Such it turned out to be, for more than £180,000 were raised. I am not going into its history, as that would take up too much time and space. The Rev. L. H. Wiseman's Introductory Statement in the Report, issued when the Fund was closed, was everything to be desired. It was a busy time with me then, for I had all the money to acknowledge and pay into our bankers, and to carry through the press the 157 pages of contributions. As soon as that was ended the Annual Report had to be taken in hand, so that I had many months of pearl-type work. Munificent gifts characterised the movement. All Methodism took part in the great undertaking.

The death of the venerable William Toase ought not to be overlooked. He was a fine old man, and had spent his life for the spiritual benefit of France, beginning with the French prisoners in the hulks in the Medway, early last century.

A new and valuable work on Fiji was recently published by Dr. Seemann, the eminent naturalist. As a disinterested and scientific witness of our work there, his testimony is the more valuable. It was most favourable to the Mission. His personal recital to the King of Hanover of what he had seen so greatly interested that monarch that he presented £100 to the Mission, and articles of value to Thakombau, the principal chief.

1864

Early in the year our missionary at Turk's Island told us of the destruction of the Mission house, chapel, and schoolroom at Puerto Plata, by the Spaniards, who stole the furniture and fired the premises. " A large number of Spanish Bibles and hymn-books, and many copies of Dr.

Rule's *Commentary on the Gospels*, were destroyed. St. Domingo is a nominally Christian country, and the Spanish people profess to believe in Christ. And yet the unoffending missionary has been driven away, the church and schools have been closed, the congregations scattered, the Mission property seized as spoils of war, and the premises wantonly and entirely destroyed. The Government of Spain refuses to allow missionaries to labour there, while native Spaniards have been severely punished for selling Bibles. And now Spain has sent her soldiers to St. Domingo, who have destroyed the only scriptural Mission in that unhappy country." Spain has long been filling up the measure of her iniquities, and she has already begun to reap what she had sown. In ancient times Spain was the first power in Europe, and now—how has the mighty fallen !

Very gloomy apprehensions were being entertained as to the results of the war in New Zealand between the English and the natives. Our missionary wrote, that " many lives will be sacrificed on both sides before the present strife is brought to a close there can be no doubt, but I do not think, as many appear to anticipate, that the streets of Auckland are to be the scene of fire and slaughter at the hands of enraged savages." Later news told of the submission of the New Zealand rebels. The particulars may not, at this distant period, be of any very great interest, but, at the time of which

I am writing, the events in that far-off beautiful land excited intense feeling.

We were told of the celebration of the Jubilee of our Missions in all parts of the world where we have Missions, and how it was taken up with great enthusiasm.

The *Quarterly Papers* for June gave the glad news of the defeat and retreat of the blood-thirsty King of Dahomey, following his attack on Abbeokuta. Many of the enemy were slain, and many taken prisoners. The hand of God was very visible here.

Our missionary at Thaba 'Nchu, in a long communication to the Committee, has this sentence: "The principal heads of the tribe came to beg me to write to the Boer authorities, whose subjects had been appropriating to themselves for some years the Barolong lands. . . . Poor people! they deserved better than this at the Boers' hands."

The Hudson's Bay Mission continued to engage attention, and the *Canada Christian Guardian* had a very interesting article on the work there. "Not - the least of the benefits of Wesleyan missionary effort in the Hudson's Bay Territory are those resulting from the translation of Scripture, hymns, etc. . . . We should not omit stating that several of our missionaries aided in Indian translation, and that the late Rev. James Evans, before named, was the sole inventor of the syllabic characters, as well as a translator; of the result

of whose genius other Churches have availed themselves. In this character we have a copy of the
entire Scriptures, printed by the Bible Society in
London; and a beautiful production it is, which
must be a source of untold blessings to those distant tribes. . . . We are of opinion that the syllabic
of the lamented and gifted James Evans will be
the prevailing channel of readable thought while
the Cree needs to be taught ' the wonderful works
of God.' "

1865

The treatment which a shipwrecked crew
would have received in former years from the
Fijians, contrasts strongly with that shown in
the following narrative by one of the survivors:—
The *All Serene*, a Sydney ship, was capsized in the
South Seas, and many on board were lost. The
survivors, in a patched-up boat, made their way
to Kandavu. Upon landing, the natives hid themselves, thinking the new-comers were slavers; but,
says the writer · " We succeeded in attracting the
attention of one of the natives, and in a few
minutes many gathered round us. None of us
could speak a word of their language, neither
could we understand anything they said, with the
exception of one word,—it was the word ' missionary'; but this word made us feel perfectly safe.
They conducted us to a small village, leading and
supporting us all the way, and seeming to vie

with each other in their unremitting attentions to us. They took us to their houses, and seemed to anticipate our every wish." The account speaks very highly of the kindness of Mr. Nettleton and Mr. Fletcher, who took care of the survivors for two months, till they obtained passages for them to Sydney.

The regret felt throughout the Society at the death of the President of the Conference, the Rev. W. L. Thornton, during his term of office, was fully shared by the Missionary Committee and throughout the entire Mission field. He was an earnest defender and zealous supporter of Missions. In meetings of the Committee his counsels were sagacious, and his manner cordial and pleasant.

The Report of the Government Inspector of Schools at Jaffna was very gratifying. He said: "I heartily congratulate the Superintendent of the Wesleyan Mission (the Rev. John Kilner) on the success which has attended his efforts in this direction,—labours of which it is impossible to speak but in terms of unmixed and unqualified approbation."

A calamity befell our Mission property at Swellendam, in the Cape Colony, when a disastrous fire broke out in the midst of a hurricane scarcely paralleled in the annals of the colony. In barely an hour's time property valued at £30,000 was destroyed. Our chapel and Mission house, with their contents, shared the same fate.

Who would have dreamt years ago of a Protestant address like the following being published in an Italian periodical? "Blessed be God, who moved you . . . whereby you were put in mind of those who in Italy were living in the shadow of death. . . . The Spirit of the Lord inclined you to come to our succour, and that Spirit kindled in you a fire of charity which sees no obstacles. . Great are the sacrifices which you have made for us. Thanks, therefore, be rendered to you in Christ, the rewarder of the saints in glory; and thanks also from us, free men and ransomed citizens, whom bonds and laws did not permit to form ourselves into churches, which are part of the Body of Christ." With much more to the same effect.

The Jamaica insurrection, which broke out in the later part of this year, is painful reading. Discontent had been growing for years, its chief cause being the poverty of the people. Since their release from slavery they had become, from their altered condition, remarkably prolific. "Sugar, the grand staple of the export trade, cannot be cultivated to advantage without scientific appliances, that is, without capital; and capital had for years been leaving Jamaica, till only 30,000 persons are now maintained by the sugar cultivation. To this population, over-numerous, poverty-stricken and ignorant, the Jamaica Legislative Assembly added a large number of coloured immigrants imported from India. . . . That Assembly is elected by less than 2500 voters in a population of 440,000, and legislates exclusively in the interest of the planters." All this helped to make the discontent more intense. The insurrection was sternly suppressed. The troops were for a while under the command of two very young English officers, whose modes of action were strongly condemned. Many innocent persons suffered during this reign of military law, and the Government was sharply called to task by right-minded persons. One of the officers was removed, so strong was the feeling.

1866

The disastrous wreck of the *London* in the Bay of Biscay, on the 11th of January, with the loss of the Rev. D. J. and Mrs. Draper, and nearly all the passengers and crew, cast a gloom over all Methodism. At the same time there was a feeling of thankfulness that Mr. Draper had been able to work for the Master up to the last moment of his life. We little thought, when he bade us good-bye at the Mission House, that he would so soon be called to his reward. But I am sure he would have asked for no other end than to die preaching the gospel and pointing sinners to the Saviour.

The death of the Rev. Robert Young was announced early in the year. He served the Society well, first as a missionary in Jamaica for ten years, as a deputation to the same island in 1843, and to the southern world in 1852. He was an able advocate of Missions all his life. Was elected President of the Conference in 1856.

An old acquaintance of mine, Dr. De Wolfe, told of the noble Sackville Academy, originated by the munificence of Mr. C. F. Allison, in New Brunswick, being destroyed by fire early in the year. From a long drought no water was to be had, and in two hours the valuable building was a mass of smouldering ruins.

The wreck of our Mission ship, the *John Wesley*, was attended by a very remarkable occurrence. " After getting on to the reef and breaking her back, she was lifted clean over the reef by a succession of immense waves, caused by an earthquake, into shallow water. The wreck was total, but our lives, and all the ship's cargo, were by this special favour from God placed out of serious danger. Oh that men would praise the Lord for His goodness to us in our trouble." A letter in the *Times* from a Boston captain corroborated the fact of the earthquake.

Later in the year it was stated in the *Notices*: " While we regret the loss of the *John Wesley*, we rejoice in the prospect of a larger and more commodious vessel to supply its place." Mr. J. J. Lidgett rendered most valuable service in connection with the new ship.

Our beautiful chapel at Nassau, in the Bahamas, was destroyed by a terrible hurricane which devastated the neighbouring islands.

Again the noble Bible Society came to the front, this time with a gift of 925 Fijian New Testaments. Who can tell the blessed result of such a gift!

1867

Good news was published in the January *Notices*, namely, that 160 Africans had been baptized in our chapel at Kamastone. It was described as a scene which the oldest missionaries in South Africa scarcely dared hope to live to witness.

Dr. M'Cosh, of Belfast, was one of the preachers and speakers at the Missionary Anniversary. The Lord Mayor of London presided. Mr. Tombleson, of Barton-on-Humber, gave £150 towards an edition of 5000 copies of the *Pilgrim's Progress* in Fijian. Where has not this immortal work penetrated!

Referring to the fearful hurricane before noticed, the missionary wrote: "Allow me on behalf of this Circuit to tender a thousand thanks to the subscribers of the Relief Fund for their timely aid. But for their beneficence our chapels must have remained in ruins, and the work of God in all its departments have suffered." Methodists are never appealed to in vain.

Another item in the *Notices* is the description

of a pretty scene given by one of the missionaries in Fiji. " On the morrow, as we sat at breakfast, we heard, faintly sounding in the distance, the first notes of a strange wild chant, growing ever louder and louder. Then amidst the green bushes we caught glimpses of the school-children slowly coming on, their little feet keeping time to the song they were singing, their heads powdered with scraped sandalwood, their well-oiled bodies adorned with garlands of leaves and flowers, and their hands bearing aloft yams, bananas, or sugar - cane, to present to us. So they came on, singing, ' This is the token of our love to the two missionaries,' " etc. The Rev. Jesse Carey wrote from Rewa : " Often have I gone to the chief of the Sabeto tribe, to beg him to become a Christian ; but I got nothing but point-blank refusals. Strange to tell, however, he came a few weeks ago to the town where I live, and while there declared for the Christian religion. The first time I preached in his town my congregation consisted of two persons, the second time a hundred, and the third time three hundred heard me preach the ' Word of Life.' "

A calamitous fire recently destroyed the town of Basseterre, in St. Kitts, which—reduced 5000 persons to homelessness and comparative destitution, and a large amount of aid was required to relieve the prevailing distress.

An inexplicable outburst of heathen savagery took place in one of the Fijian group of islands, in the murder of one of our valued missionaries, the Rev. Thomas Baker, and six of our native agents, while on a missionary tour. It was a cruel and altogether unprovoked crime. The acting consul for Fiji, in a communication to the Colonial Secretary, expressed his opinion that Thakombau would deal out justice to the murderers.

1868

The January *Notices* tell of an unusual series of calamities which had befallen several parts of the Mission field. In Abbeokuta there had been a violent outburst of popular fury, which culminated in the expulsion of our two missionaries and the temporary suspension of the Mission. At Tortola, in the West Indies, there was a fearful hurricane, doing terrible mischief; and other disasters were reported.

The Universal Exhibition at Paris had a large show of missionary items, lent by our own and other Societies, and for seven months the agents in charge were busily employed in giving information. The *Moniteur Universel* had a commendatory article on the Wesleyan part of the missionary exhibition.

The death of the Rev. John Scott took place this year, after a ministry of fifty-seven years. For many years he had been one of the General Treasurers, and much regret was felt at his death. Another of our prominent ministers, Dr. Hannah, soon followed his old friend Mr. Scott to his reward. They had both been Presidents of the Conference.

1869

Good news reached us early this year from Antigua, when our missionary told us that, "So far, there have been nearly 700 conversions in this Circuit, and about 230 on trial. A great and wonderful change has passed upon a large section of the population in each of our stations. I believe this is but the beginning of better days. We shall see greater things than these."

The Rev. Samuel Dalzell bears testimony to the high value which many of the Hindus are beginning to put on the Bible, evinced in their eagerness to buy it, in the earnestness with which they read it, and in the anxiety which they manifest that their children should be taught it.

It was pleasing to see that the Society's financial statement, given at the Annual Meeting, contained the handsome gift of £200 from the King of Holland for the St. Martin's and St. Eustatius Missions in the West Indies; also nearly £100 from the Emperor of the French for St. Martin's. These gifts were repeated in following years.

This was a cruel year, for three lamentable deaths by violence were reported. The Rev. James Caldwell was accidentally drowned after but two years' missionary service for his Master in China. The Rev. John Whiteley, while on his way to visit a settler whom he had been in the habit of visiting, was passing through the bush when suddenly five Maori rifles flashed, and five balls bore instant death to one of the oldest and truest friends of the Maori people, whose face and name were known to almost every native along the western coast.　Seven other white persons had been murdered in the same neighbourhood during the day.　His ministry extended from 1831 to 1869.　The third was that of the Rev. W. Hill. He was visiting as chaplain the prisoners at Pentridge, in Melbourne, when he was barbarously murdered by one of the prisoners, who is supposed to have been for the time insane.

A short extract from an Indian missionary at Bangalore is worth quoting, showing the immense difficulties of the work of evangelising India. "With the Hindus the intellectual difficulties are great.　We who have been brought up in the midst of Christian influences cannot appreciate how great they are.　The whole doctrine of the Atonement is a perplexity. . . . In the case of a Hindu the conviction of sin must be very deep before he will become a Christian. . . . When urging a young Hindu to become a Christian, we are pressing him to expose himself to trials and persecutions which we ourselves have never borne, and is enough to fill us with deep emotion and sympathy.　The grief and despair of many a Hindu parent if his son became a Christian would be as great as that of a devout Christian if his son became a pervert to Mohammedanism, while it would be unrelieved by the faith and hope of the gospel."

One of our native teachers tells of a perilous visit he made to a heathen tribe in the interior part of Rewa. On presenting himself to the chief, he said, "Look you! We have taken counsel, we kill folk, and my word has gone forth throughout all the mountains—that the man who comes here bringing the *lotu*, whoever he may be, whether missionary or teacher, is to be brought here that I may eat him. This is my word. And now you have brought us into a strait by your coming. What am I to do? The other tribes will say I have befooled them. Why did you come, teacher; why did you come? Three times have we sat in council about you, and nothing is determined upon yet. But you shall live. Go now; the drum is yours. Beat it for your preaching on the morrow."

The death of Mr. J. J. Lidgett was a great loss to Methodism and to our Missions. He was a wise counsellor in the Society's operations, and succeeded Mr. Irving of Bristol in attending to the affairs of our missionary ship, the *John Wesley*. He married the daughter of the Rev. John Scott. His very worthy brother, Mr. George Lidgett, who still survives, married Mr. Scott's other daughter.

1870

The January *Notices* begin thus: — "It is a matter of devout thankfulness to be able to inaugurate the new year with joyful news from the East. India and China, with their countless populations, bewildering mythologies, gigantic idolatries, and licentious rites, will severely tax the faith, patience, and energies of all the Christian Churches; and it is indeed cause for much rejoicing when, in the heat of the formidable struggle, the friends of Christ are cheered by some first-fruits of the coming victory."

The Rev. John Scott, of the Ceylon Mission, reports the spreading of the remarkable revival of religion there. He writes: "500 conversions in four months rejoice and, at the same time, humble me to the dust." Mr. Baugh writes: "Praise God for ever! Heaven will not lack trophies of the Saviour's power, even from the land of Buddhism; hundreds, thousands of sainted Singhalese, believers in Jesus, will greet us in that blessed land."

Again has poor Hayti come to the front; this time by a disastrous civil war, when the capital, Port au Prince, was bombarded, and nearly half the place burnt down, including our entire Mission property there: the church, a brick-and-stone building, Mission house, and property. Mr. Bird wrote: "Hayti, like too many other nations, has sought and served everything and anything but

God; and she has long been reaping that which she has long been sowing, until she has made it evident that ' the wages of sin is death.'"

The Rev. W. Shepstone, writing from Kamastone of the native agents whom God had raised up, says : " I have listened to their eloquence with delight, especially on one occasion not long since, when, under a Divine influence, a large congregation, to which one of these was preaching, was bowed and swayed like the trees of the forest before a mighty wind. . . . How well they knew how to reach the inmost recesses and workings of the native mind! Mr. Shaw, Mr. Boyce, and myself can now look back and contemplate more correctly—and, as I have little fear but we shall, with deeper emotion than any who have entered this native field of labour at a much later date—the two standpoints of 1830 and of 1870."

Who did not like Thomas Vasey ? There was such an openness in him, such wit, that he drew people to him. He was one of our City Road preachers, and we often had him at Hackney Road. He was much at the Mission House on business, and was very friendly with me. He spoke at the Annual Meeting this year. One part of his speech was so neatly put that I cannot refrain from quoting it. He said: " I do not know how it is, or by what wonderful art of combination, all the speakers, who have no communication with each other, so dilate that the speeches altogether form beautiful specimens of mosaic work, which you might have thought to be the work of one man who had chosen the colours and pattern and blended them artistically together, so as to produce the best possible effect. I am sure that no kind of forethought or skill or pre-arrangement could have produced a better assortment of speeches and a better harmony of topics than those which have been presented to us under some mysterious and plastic and inspiring influence at this meeting." Mr. Vasey's ministry lasted from 1839 to 1871.

The Missions on the Continent of Europe were greatly paralysed by the breaking out of war between France and Germany. Several of the German ministers were called from their evangelical work to perform military service in the Prussian lines. My heart ached as I read of the disasters which befell both nations, and I often cried out, "Poor France!"

This year's announcements must be wound up with one which sent a thrill of joy into the hearts of all right-thinking Christians. "The event for which Italian patriots and earnest Protestants have for years been looking has at length been suddenly and mysteriously realised. The temporal power has been wrenched from the reluctant hands of Pius IX., and the Eternal City, with its surrounding States, has been absorbed into the united kingdom of Victor Emmanuel. With this great event I delight to associate the name of one of the world's greatest patriots, Garibaldi. All honour to his memory!

Mr. Piggott wrote from Rome early in the year: "Here in this city of Rome, under the shadow of the great Basilica . . . it has been freely discussed between Catholics and Protestants, by chosen champions on both sides, *whether Peter was ever in Rome at all.*"

1871

Lord Lawrence, late Viceroy and Governor-General of India, kindly took the chair at the Highbury Missionary Meeting, and spoke in high commendation of Mission work in India. "Not only did the missionaries expose their health and wear away their strength in struggling in a distant country among a strange people, but in many cases their lives were held in their hands; and in some cases, to his knowledge, they had laid down their lives, after having in the course of years done everything they could, directly and indirectly, in religious and secular things, to benefit the people among whom they had laboured. . . . He could recollect the day when a missionary could not live in the city of Lahore, and no Englishman could resort there without an armed escort; but now Sunday schools were established, and missionaries were looked up to with respect and gratitude by many individuals among that population."

"An eligible site for the erection of a church and

school in Naples having been offered, the Secretaries were authorised by the Committee to negotiate for the purchase of it. The immediate occupation of Rome was the subject of a lengthened conversation, after which it was resolved that an Italian minister should be at once sent there." What must King Bomba and Pope Pius have thought of this— Methodist services under their very noses! These kingdoms had been long enough under the rule of the priest.

The Committee might well write in the May *Notices*: "It is with no ordinary exultation and thankfulness that we announce to our friends the opening of a Wesleyan Methodist preaching-place within the walls of Rome."

The Rev. John Watsford, President of the Australian Conference at Hobart Town, told of his work in Fiji years before. He said he had seen more that was true and sincere among the natives than he had seen elsewhere. "In Fiji to-day (1871) there were 100,000 professing Christians, and as good professing Christians as those in Hobart Town (where he was speaking) or elsewhere."

Mr. John Chubb took the chair at the Exeter Hall Meeting this year. He was another among many whom I deeply regarded and respected. I remember his father, Mr. Charles Chubb,—in fact, all the family,—and was brought much into contact with them. The son was a liberal man, and a deep lover of Missions. He once played a trick on the Methodist agitators. The Rev. J. P. Dunn was appointed to preach at Long Lane Chapel, and Mr. Chubb sent an advertisement to the *Times*: " To Methodist Reformers.—The Rev. Mr. Dunn will preach (naming the chapel and time); all Methodist Reformers urged to attend." It was a " sell," for it was not the Reformer Dunn.

Mr. Fernley, of Southport, founder of the " Fernley Lectures," most generously offered £5000 towards a place of worship in Rome; and Mr. Heald offered the same amount for the same object and towards the Society's debt, which was gradually rolling away.

Our missionary at Tonga wrote: " The Roman Catholic Church is the *enemy* of the Tongan Government. When we call to mind the circumstances under which it commenced its history and made its first converts, and remember the unyielding and uncompromising character of the papacy, we are justified in calling it the enemy of the Tongan nation."

CHAPTER VIII

A MISSIONARY RETROSPECT, 1872–1882

1872

THE January *Notices* begin with : " We have much pleasure in calling attention to the interest taken by Lord Napier, the Governor of Madras, in the work of Missions generally, and in the educational department in particular. It is a favourable sign for India when its rulers favour the spread of Christianity and of true civilisation, in place of the gross idolatry and barbarous customs which have for ages tyrannised over the inhabitants of that country."

Special subscriptions for the Mission to Rome and for the extinction of the Society's debt were received, amounting to nearly £25,000. What a spirit of liberality came upon our people at that time! Mr. J. S. Budgett and Mr. Arthur acted as a deputation to the North of England to urge these claims.

Earnest prayer was made in Committee for the recovery of the Prince of Wales from an all but fatal illness. I well remember the agony of mind we suffered as the papers told us daily of the Prince's sad state. The truly venerable Dr. Dixon's death took place this year. He was for a time one of the Society's missionaries, and for many years one of its most eloquent advocates.

Referring to the death of Tamata Waka Nene, or, in English, Thomas Walker, we were told that he was the firm friend of the English in former years, and honourable mention was made of him by the Governor of the colony. He died full of years. What a change had passed over New Zealand in fifty years! The land was entirely heathen, savage, and cannibal—no churches, no schools, no books. Now the Scriptures are translated into the native tongue, and the Bible Society has furnished 10,000 copies of the New Testament. Nearly the whole population can read; schools and chapels are provided for the use of the people. Missions have not failed here.

At the Canadian Missionary Anniversary, Dr. Punshon spoke in a style which showed that the fire and flow of his platform eloquence had not abated, that he held Foreign Missionary enterprise essential to the conservation and development of the life of Home Churches.

The Committee received " with feelings of devout gratitude " the intelligence of the formation of a branch of the Bible Society in Rome. The death of Mr. J. Robinson Kay removed a well-known and most liberal Methodist. His name was almost a "household word." We had him on special Committee gatherings now and then at the Mission House. I used to look on the holders of these well-known names with interest and respect.

The August *Notices* begin thus: "Death has imposed upon us a mournful duty. The 'right hand' which so often wrote the Introduction to the *Notices* has forgotten its 'cunning.' The venerable and much-loved Dr. Hoole, after a short illness, entered the everlasting rest on Monday, June 17th, in the seventy-fifth year of his age."

Thanks were given to the Committee for the " Propagation of the Gospel " for kindly forwarding an extract from the early proceedings of the Society, referring to the Rev. John Wesley while their missionary in Georgia.

"The attention of all Christian Churches has of late been largely concentrated on the Continent of Europe, and many hopes have been cherished that recent events may create fresh opportunities for the spread of Protestant Christianity. The Franco-German War, the dreadful horrors of the Commune in Paris, and the sudden overthrow of the Napoleonic dynasty, have helped to strengthen a conviction in many thoughtful Frenchmen that there is no security for individuals, or for nations, except in the kingdom which cannot be moved."

1873

Our Italian missionary, Francesco Sciarelli, issued a " Pastoral " to the Methodists of Rome, which reminds one of the " Epistles " of apostolic times.   One sentence is worth quoting: " O my Methodist brethren of Rome, abide firm in the faith to which, by my feeble voice, the Lord has called you! Testify of Jesus Christ before a corrupt world, and be ye that ' handful of corn in the earth upon the top of the mountains,' the fruit whereof shall be great." This was replied to by a Romish daily in this fashion " The Protestants will not understand that without a religious authority, without a Pope, faith in the supernatural is impossible ' to the Government.' Do you see what you have come to Rome to do? To sow schism and heresy. You have caused the Methodist place for religious perversion to be planted in face of the *Vicariat*, as if in scorn of its head," etc.

The death of the very venerable Thomas Jackson was reported to the Committee on March 12th. Few men were venerated more by me.

Mr. Spurgeon kindly preached for the Society one of its Missionary Sermons, described as eminently characteristic—full of noble sentiments and rich in holy unction. Good news was announced at the meeting, of the entire extinguishing of the Society's debt, and that 1500 members had been added to the Mission churches. Their joy was chastened by the removal of three of the noblest standard - bearers, Elijah Hoole, William Shaw, and Thomas Jackson. The address of the noble chairman, Lord Napier, was especially valuable as the testimony of an independent observer to the importance of Christian Missions in India.

The *South Sea Bubbles* was a book written by an English earl and his companion, a doctor, by no means favourable to missionary operations in the South Seas. Our missionary wrote that he " wondered very much that the writers did not visit some at least of the ten missionary districts into which the islands are divided, as men intending to write a book ought to have done. I never heard of their visiting Mission stations or travelling with the missionaries in their canoes from which they would have been able to write correctly as to the actual work done, and the reformation that had been effected."

We read in the October *Notices* that " the Ashantee hordes are in possession of the open country, and have burnt most of our chapels and schoolrooms in the general destruction of property which follows their invasion."

In the December *Notices* the death of Mr. Heald, the Society's Treasurer, is announced, and the Committee recorded their loss in the following words : " In the first Report of the Society, dated 1818, Mr. Heald's name is found among the subscribers. From that time onwards his support has been constantly given to it, and for many years he and his family have stood in the front rank of its benefactors. When special occasions arose to call for the united efforts of the Methodist Connexion, either to relieve the Society from embarrassment or to provide means for extending its operations, he repeatedly afforded special assistance and encouragement. A long list of such occasions, were it needful to recount them, would be fittingly closed with his noble gift of £5000 in aid of the extension of Methodism in Italy   The Committee regard Mr. Heald's removal as a bereavement unusually afflictive, and a loss which cannot easily be repaired."

The death of the Rev. Henry Wharton was a severe blow to the Gold Coast Mission, where he was Chairman of the District for several years. He died at Madeira, on his way to England.

1874

What a curse and what a hindrance to the work of God in China is opium! What souls and bodies of the Chinese it has ruined! What a disgrace to us, that our Government derives so large an income from it, while we, a professedly Christian nation, send missionaries to teach our religion. I suppose the natives do not discriminate between the doings of our Government and those of individual societies. Anyhow, it is a national disgrace.

The accounts we read of the opium dens, both here in the East End of London and elsewhere, are horrible in the extreme. " Opium is eating out the very life of the nation, physically and morally, among both high and low, and the ungodly lives of foreigners cause the adorable name of Jesus to be every day blasphemed among the heathen."

Our chairman of the Queen's Town District, the Rev. W. J. Davis, was complimented by the Colonial Government for his literary labours in preparing a Kaffir Grammar and Dictionary, copies of which were to be placed in all the offices of the native department. They also made him a grant of £100.

One must read in full the account sent home by Mr. Gillings, of Madras, of the trials endured by our young native converts in their efforts to break away from the worship of their heathen idols,— how fathers and mothers have gone on their knees to implore their sons not to forsake the religion of their ancestors; how the aid of the magistrate has been invoked; what false swearing as to age; and the danger to the missionary from infuriated mobs led on by members of the convert's family. It is painful but encouraging reading.

An account of Thakombau, King of Fiji, is given in the May *Notices*. The missionary says: " At the very first interview in 1850 he refused permission for me to reside at Bau. On that occasion he could well have been compared to Lucifer for pride.

He was almost naked; his face was painted up to the eyes; his massive head of hair covered with a gauze turban; his beard was of great length; his eyes looked bloodthirsty. A score of armed men, who all looked like professional cut-throats, followed closely at his heels." Early in 1854 this barbarian yielded to the force of truth, backed by the entreaties of his faithful missionary, idolatry was publicly disowned, and permission given to renounce the old worship and embrace Christianity.

I like to look through Dr. Punshon's speeches at the Exeter Hall Meetings. Speeches? They were orations! No wonder people hung on his words. This was well put at this year's meeting, the first after his return from his seven years' residence in Canada: "How comes it, that England, when the revolutionary deluge submerged so many places, never wavered? Why, because, while France, unhappy France, was drifting into infidelity, England stayed herself sublimely in her faith; and in the principles of the gospel of the Lord Jesus Christ she found her safety and her strength." Then the Doctor drew his hearers to the graves of those who had joined the hosts of heaven, of the valiant warders who were accustomed to meet with them in former days, enumerating their names. How well the orator could do this we all knew.

The death of the Rev. Emile F. Cook was a loss to our Mission in France. He was President of the French Conference. In one of his journeys he was shipwrecked, by the vessel colliding with the *Ville du Havre,* and being so damaged that 87 out of 313 passengers had to be taken off by another ship. Mr. Cook would not leave the ill-fated vessel, staying on board to nurse a brother minister who was injured and unable to move. But signs of sinking soon showed, and the sufferers were removed by the *British Queen* just before the injured vessel sank. The sufferings he went through brought on inflammation, and in a very few months he was called home, leaving a widow and seven children. He had passed through the twofold siege of Paris.

1875

The Governor of the Gold Coast, we were told, assembled the Gold Coast chieftains and addressed them in words of wisdom. He reminded them of the protection they had received from the British Government, and required submission and obedience to the Queen's regulations. " In return for the benefits conferred upon you," said the Governor, "the Queen requests your aid in putting an end to a thing that she and her people abhor. This thing is against a law which no king or queen of England can ever change. . . . The English people do not buy men, women, and children. The Queen is determined to put a stop at once to the buying of slaves within or without the Protectorate." This was firm language, much to be commended. The February *Notices* tell us of the deposition of the King of Ashantee, Coffee-Karri-Karri, by his chiefs; and the fact of his dismissal, without injury to private life, are creditable traits in the Ashantee character.

The sad news of the death of the Rev. Luke H. Wiseman soon spread, causing deep sorrow, for he was a man much beloved and a pillar in our Church. I very highly respected him, and had much to do with him in connection with the Jubilee of the Missionary Society.

Early this year a large deputation from the Missionary Committee waited on Sir A. H. Gordon, K.C.M.G., the first Governor of Fiji; for, chiefly through the persistent efforts of Sir W. M'Arthur, the islands had been annexed by the British Government. The object of the deputation was mainly to assure the worthy Governor of their sympathy and prayers, "hoping that during his administration the benefits of our civilisation would be conveyed to Fiji, unaccompanied by the injurious consequences which too often follow in its train."

What instances of great liberality our Society has had to record! Here is one worth noting: "John Wilson, Esq., Waterford, in accordance with the wishes of his late brother, Thomas Wilson, Esq., £7000."

Referring to our work in Bohemia, a speaker at Exeter Hall said· "I have a sort of dim vision before me of a wonderful apostolic succession in connection with that land of Bohemia. Shall I give you the links of it?——John Huss, Christian David, Count Zinzendorf, Peter Bohler, and John Wesley; there is no break in the chain either. Now, I think we owe something to Bohemia."

Testimony was borne to the value of our Missions in South Africa by an independent· witness, T. L. Phipson, Esq., to a friend. " During our extended tour we met with many missionaries, and remained for some time at their several stations. I was therefore enabled to see for myself the good that accrued from their residence amongst the wildest of Africa's children. Of the many denominations to be met with upon the frontier, the Wesleyan Missionary Society has by far the greater number of stations, and as a rule they are the most important." The writer goes on to particularise several of the Mission stations.

By some misfortune, the plague of measles, supposed to have been imported from Sydney, broke out in the Fiji group, resulting in that country passing through a terribly severe ordeal. Whole villages were prostrated at once. One missionary wrote: " The visitation has been more like that of cholera or plague than measles as *you* understand it." Anyone who can at all realise the condition of a semi-civilised people like this, their habits, ignorance, kind of food, and mode of getting it, must expect great mortality. The mortality amounted to many thousands, and the country was panic-stricken.

1876

The January *Notices* report the death of the Kaffir chief Kama, aged seventy-six years. He was one of the first converts to Christianity, under the ministry of the Rev. Wm. Shaw. He had been a member of the Wesleyan Society more than fifty years, and was loyal to the British Government through the three Kaffir wars.

The Australian Conference last year commenced a mission to the Duke of York's Island, New Britain, etc. It was a wise thing to hand over to that Conference the work which was inviting their labours in those far-away lands. This was the natural result of the formation of the Australian Conferences. Our missionary, on his way to these places, on board the *John Wesley* wrote: "What is before us? What trials, what rejoicings? How many fights, how many victories? How long before these people receive the gospel and rejoice in the assurance of the Saviour's love?"

The Rev. Arthur Brigg, writing from Bensonvale, Bechuanaland, said: "While revolving in my mind plans of aggressive work, what was my surprise, and that of the class-leaders assembled with me in the Leaders' Meeting one day, to behold a heathen chief, with one or two retainers, painted with red clay, rubbed over with fat, and a blanket over his shoulders, from the very locality I had been thinking of, come to request that a teacher might be sent to reside at his place and preach the gospel to them!"

The Rev. G. T. Perks, having, at the request of the Committee, undertaken to visit the South African stations, did his work with a will; and his Journals, published in several numbers of the *Notices*, showed that it was no child's work. It was a laborious mission he was engaged in, and it told upon him. On his return I could see a change in him,—he had lost flesh. We were all glad to see him back, for we loved him. He told in his Journal, that "Krieli, the great chief of the Galekas, having heard that I was at Butterworth, came to see me, accompanied by his brother, by his favourite old general, and by one of his principal councillors. I was glad to see the chief, of whom I had read and heard so much. He has been a majestic and powerful man, but is beginning to exhibit the frailties and infirmities of age. But in conversation he soon became animated, and the fire of the old warrior flashed in his keen and restless eye. I spoke to him a few kind words, and reminded him that the missionaries had always been his best advisers."

Dr. Gervase Smith at the Annual Meeting made graceful allusion to the noble action of Dean Stanley in connection with the monument in

Westminster Abbey to the memory of John and Charles Wesley. It was a pleasure to me to supply the artist, Mr. Adams (Acton), with some portraits and models for his use in executing his beautiful memorial; and he kindly "took" me in clay and inserted me as one of Wesley's hearers.

The sad death of the Rev. G. M'Dougall, who perished in a snowstorm while carrying the blest Evangel to the perishing Indians in the North-Western Territory, was announced. "The manner of his death, though painful, was a fitting close to his self-denying life. No friends soothed his last hours, or gathered up the words of trustful prayer that fell from his dying lips. Like Moses, he died alone with God."

One of our best Methodist antiquarians, the Rev. S. R. Hall, this year joined the great majority. What a collection of Wesleyana he had! It was partly lent by members of the family for exhibition in the Allan Library at the Centenary of Wesley's death. Dr. Waddy's death was also announced in the December *Notices*. Both he and Mr. Hall were ex-Presidents. The Rev. Alfred Barrett, our pastor for three years at Hackney Road, also passed away at this time. His earnest ministry for this period was long remembered.

1877

The *Windsor Castle*, with five missionaries on board, went ashore on a barren island about thirty-five miles from Cape Town, fortunately without loss of life or baggage ; but until the passengers were rescued their sufferings were severe from cold and exposure. The account of the disaster adds · " I cannot conclude without stating how deep is the feeling that we all share, that we were under the special providence of Almighty God, and that His interposition is most plainly seen."

The Rev. Dr. Stamp's death brought forth from the Committee an expression of sincere respect for him. He was one of the most gentlemanly persons I knew, and was an occasional correspondent with me.

A fine large painting of Dr. Waddy was presented to the Mission House by Mr. S. D. Waddy (afterwards Judge Waddy). It was a speaking likeness, and was a valuable addition to our Methodist " Valhalla."

Mr. Waddy took the chair at the Exeter Hall Meeting this year. His speech on the occasion was a grand missionary oration, and that meeting was one of our best.

By a strange mysterious providence, we were called upon to mourn over the death of the Rev. G. T. Perks, whose sudden decease sent a thrill through our church. I little thought, when he bade me good-morning on the Saturday mid-day, that he would be numbered with the dead on the following Monday. He died in the prime f life : few men more beloved.

The trials of native converts in India we in favoured England cannot realise. Mr. Hocken tells of one, a tall handsome boy, remarkable for his intelligence and decision of character. When he took the final step by being baptized, his father and brothers received him with a storm of abuse; it was fearful to hear the awful imprecations with which his father greeted him. The youth was connected with some of the best families in the place. Things reached a climax when about two hundred Brahmins came armed with clubs to the Mission house, shouting and cursing. A charge was made against the missionary at the Deputy Commissioner's Court at Mysore of kidnapping the youth, but it was shown that the lad was an entirely free agent in the case. He beautifully said, while under severe cross-examination, " Before I gave myself to Christ I was an unclean outcast, but now I am a Brahmin of the purest type."

1878

As South Africa is so much to the front at present (1902), the following extract from the Rev. G. Blencowe may possess interest: " The Transvaal is intrinsically the best part of Her Majesty's dominions in South Africa. It has a greater range of climate and of agricultural capability than any other South African colony. Its mineral wealth is great and various; iron, copper, lead, coal, and gold abound. The characteristics of the country make it popular among all South African residents, so that nearly one half of the farms . . . have been purchased by their present owners since the opening of the gold-fields. The extent of good land for farming purposes is so great that it may double its present number of inhabitants every five years for a century, and leave plenty of room for those who come after A.D. 2000."

After many and strange adventures David Magatta found his way to Thaba 'Nchu, where, soon after his arrival, he sought and found salvation, and began at once to exhort others to seek the Lord. He was formally appointed to this work by the Rev. W. Shaw. After a while he felt constrained to visit his birthplace to tell them of the Saviour. Then he went to Potchefstroom, where he besought, exhorted, and commanded them to repent. For this the landrost sentenced him to a public whipping in the street with the cat, and then banished him. He went to Natal for a short time, and afterwards fell in with Paul Kruger, at that time a commandant of the Republic, who gave him a written authorisation to return to Potchefstroom and teach the people, and preach the gospel to them, forbidding any man to hinder him. This was very praiseworthy of the now dethroned President.

At the General Committee Meeting of June

17th "a MS. of a Zulu Dictionary, prepared by the Rev. C. Roberts, of Natal, having been presented to the Committee, and strongly recommended by the Natal District Meeting as a most valuable work, and one that will be of essential service in the future working of vernacular educational and evangelistic plans in that part of Africa, the Committee resolves that it be printed," etc.

The death of Mr. E. T. Eyton, of Kingstown, was announced. This gentleman, under the initials of E. T. E. and T. E. E., had given to the Society's funds the large amount of £28,000 during the last thirty-three years. We looked anxiously from time to time for his helpful gifts, always paid in at our bankers.

Our missionary in Fingoland tells of a tribal war breaking out between the Galekas and Fingoes, the former pouring in such a horde of warriors that matters began to look very serious, until Sir Bartle Frere, the Governor of the colony, gave the former to understand that, as the Fingoes were British subjects, it meant war with the British; and this brought matters to a crisis.

1879

This year began jubilantly. The January *Notices* say: "The grand results of the Thanksgiving Fund meetings in London are cause for the profoundest gratitude. The Missionary Committee may reasonably calculate on the complete extinction of the debt of last year. We thank God for that."

The Rev. R. Giddy, writing from Wittebergen, says : " It is a great blessing that we have Sir Bartle Frere for our Governor and High Commissioner ;— careful, judicious, far-seeing, but nevertheless firm, and the friend both of colonists and the natives. Now, perhaps, more than ever before, it is the time for prayer to God that He would avert the evils which are hanging over us, and cause all things to work together for good." He adds : " Cetewayo, the Zulu chief, is very powerful, and I am apprehensive that the struggle will be a deadly one."

Our Sierra Leone missionary, Mr. Jope, told of hard work in these words : " The full charge of over two thousand members is of itself no mean task even in an English Circuit, but here it is considerably heightened. Everything to be done by oneself ; the far more numerous and distressing calls for the exercise of discipline, and the thousand and one other things known only to those engaged in them."

Sir Arthur Gordon, G.C.M.G., Governor of Fiji, spoke at the Annual Meeting this year. He said : " It was desired that I should give such testimony as I can afford to the work, the great and most satisfactory work, performed by the Wesleyan Missions in that remote part of the world with which I am at present connected. That testimony it affords me the highest pleasure and gratification to give." His Excellency went into many particulars connected with our Mission in Fiji. The Governor was evidently a close observer of Mission work.

" The influx of Chinese into Australia has of late caused much uneasiness, and repressive legislation is being carried in the different Legislatures to stop the immigration. Much ill-feeling has been evoked, and anti-Chinese leagues have been formed. ' John Chinaman ' is likely to have a rough time of it, and our diplomatic relations with China will no doubt be affected."

At the end of the year Mr. Kilner, one of the most valuable secretaries we ever had, started with Mrs. Kilner on a mission to South Africa. He was charged with the weighty task of visiting the South African Districts, for the purpose of making inquiries and collecting facts that will help the Committee in their future administration of those Districts.

1880

In the January *Notices* the Committee record their loss in the death of the Rev. John Rattenbury : " It glorifies God in the saintly life and richly evangelical and fruitful ministry of His servant, but it desires specially to mark its appreciation of the distinguished service which Mr. Rattenbury rendered for many years to the cause of Foreign Missions, both in Committee, in the pulpit, and on the platform."

A visit to the Jebu country by our native catechist at Abbeokuta is given in the February *Notices* ; also Mr. Milum's letter to Jaja, King of

Opobo, showing what openings there were in those benighted lands for gospel work. Mr. Milum, whom I well knew and highly respected, gave me a few very interesting curiosities from the interior for my own museum, as well as adding many to the Mission House collection.

At the Annual Meeting, among the well-spoken things by Mr. William Bickford-Smith, the chairman, was this : " The idolatry of the world has diminished more within the last fifty years than it did in the thousand years which preceded it. The destruction of idols, which is so rapidly taking place in our day, has been predicted as one of the grand events which would usher in the coming of the Lord." The Rev. James Scott, from South Africa, where he had well served his Master for twenty years, gave the testimony of Her Majesty's representative in Basutoland, who had a life-long acquaintance with the natives. " The work of forty years has not left the missionaries without valuable testimonies to the faithfulness and efficiency of their labours in this country—testimonies which consist not in elaborate reports to Societies at home, but in the religious life and Christian conduct of thousands of natives, who would otherwise be enveloped to-day in the darkness of their primitive heathenism." Such a testimony speaks volumes.

The Rev. J. C. W. Gostick, in his speech at Exeter Hall, spoke of a native preacher, Abijah Samuel, thus : " I would just pay a tribute of love to the memory of Abijah Samuel, with whom I worked and laboured about seven years. He was a remarkable native preacher, and we used to call him the 'Punshon' of India. Heathens and Christians hung upon his lips; and stern, proud Englishmen, who did not believe in the goodness of any native, believed in Abijah Samuel. . . . The Church that could raise that man from a low-born pariah and make him the greatest native Wesleyan preacher throughout all India need not fear criticism."

. A young convert from Zululand spoke at the Breakfast Meeting, the Rev. C. Roberts interpreting. Mr. Roberts told us he had left that country two years ago, and was not sure he could recollect 12,000 Zulu words, any one of which may be required by the speaker.

The missionary at Mount Charles, Jamaica, sent accounts of sad tropical hurricanes causing great damage to our property. It was but ten months before that he told us of one of the chapels being entirely destroyed by flood. The houses of the peasantry were demolished by hundreds, and scores of churches reduced to shapeless ruins. It was a terrible hurricane, not confined to Mount Charles, but it visited other parts, doing vast damage.

Sir Francis Lycett's death was reported at the end of this year. "His spirit of missionary enterprise and love of aggression led him to take great interest in the China Mission when it was first commenced, and it was he who originated what was at first called the 'China Breakfast Meeting,' but is now known as the Missionary Breakfast—an established part of the Anniversary."

1881

A lively scene is portrayed by our missionary at Porto Novo, in Western Africa, in the January *Notices.* He wrote: "At about ten minutes past three p.m. we were startled by an alarming cry of 'Fire! fire!' We all rushed out, and saw the fire blazing vehemently upon the roofs of the native thatched houses opposite and abreast of us. Unfortunately a strong wind set in, and the position of the fire changed and divided its course into three parts. The whole country was at once in great consternation; men, women with babes on their backs, and children running to and fro, up and down the street, crying out with fear. It was indeed an awful sight to behold." The people having no fire-engines, the fire gradually burned itself out. The chapel and Mission house narrowly escaped.

Dr. Jobson's death on January 4th removed from our midst a notable man. His *Life and Sermons*, edited by his widow, is a grateful monument to his memory. I well remember him in my early days. How the fire blazed in our Hackney Road pulpit when he preached! He was a man much beloved, and to our Missions a true friend. He was for twelve years one of the General Treasurers.

Mr. Whitamore, writing from Calcutta, said: " I

saw the other day an image of Ganesh (the elephant-headed idol) over a certain shop in Calcutta, and asked an intelligent young native, 'Who made it?' He said, with a look of shame, 'I, sir.' 'What is it for?' I asked; and he replied, with a confession that was pitiable, 'It is our god, sir.' 'And do you make your own gods on the premises?' 'Oh, well,' he said, in perfect English, 'I know it's all *humbug*; there is nothing in it: but our fathers did it, and so must we.' That can only last a little longer, according to the best judges; the days of Ganesh and Doorga and Kali are numbered."

The Rev. Owen Watkins, for whom I have great respect as one of our most enterprising missionaries in South Africa, as well as for his geniality, wrote under date of January 10th: "The state of the Transvaal is most sad; the whole country seems to be in the hands of the Boers. The telegraph wires have been cut, and postal communication has been stopped. At our last advices most of the towns had been taken, and both Pretoria and Standerton were threatened. . . . My heart is very sad as I contemplate the destruction for the time being of all our plans for aggressive work in the Transvaal; but my comfort is, the Lord reigneth, and He will cause even the wrath of man to praise Him."

The Society of Friends sent one of their members to the Mysore to ascertain the nature and extent of missionary work there. At the close of his communication to the Society, speaking of Wesley Samuels, one of our native pastors, he said: " His sermon and his prayer were as though he had caught the spirit of fire that inspired the early Methodists in our own country, and I could not help thinking how John Wesley would rejoice to look down and see the flame burning brightly out among these swarthy sons of the tropics. I believe a great harvest of souls awaits the thoroughgoing, methodical work of various kinds carried on hereaway by the Wesleyan Mission. May the blessing of the Lord rest abundantly upon them, and give them the riches of His harvest."

What shall be said with reference to an event that stirred all Methodism, in the death of Dr. Punshon ? It came upon us with terrible suddenness, and it was a long time before it could be realised. He was but fifty-seven years old—humanly speaking, too young to die. The death of such a man is a deep mystery. The world wanted him a little longer, and so did our Missionary Society, and so did his bereaved family   I purpose to refer to him more at length in my chapter on " Men I have Known."

Surely bloodstained Dahomey was the worst country in all God's earth ! From calculations made, Mr. Milum wrote : " I think the present King of Dahomey may be regarded as the greatest murderer living." And he urges on behalf of humanity the annexation of the whole coastline between Quetta and Lagos to the Gold Coast Colony, which, if I mistake not, has been done.

1882

The March *Notices* told us of a terrible calamity which befell our work in New Zealand, in the wreck of a vessel, when several ministers and laymen were drowned on their way from New Zealand to the Australian General Conference—a disaster long remembered.

I always had a pleasant remembrance of the Rev. Henry Bleby, both for what he did and *suffered* for the Master, for it is not every missionary who has had the honour of being tarred and feathered, as Mr. Bleby had been, by West Indian planters. He died this year, after one of the most useful and laborious lives a missionary could live.

The news from South Africa was of a very encouraging nature. Graham's Town reported an increase of 200 per cent. on the number of its members; Queen's Town told of a revival by which 280 have been brought into the fold; and in the Natal District there is a congregation of 100 Zulus, and a steady increase in numbers. We may well thank God and take courage.

An earnest appeal was made on behalf of Palermo, now rejoicing in the privileges of a free Italy. How it was that the noble Italians suffered themselves to remain under the heel of such government as they had endured time without end, is surprising.

But the end came, and light came to priest-ridden Italy, including Palermo. The appeal told us of the formation of a Sunday school, Young Men's Christian Association, evening schools, and other good work following the introduction of the gospel. Palermo is on the Minutes as a Circuit.

One of the missionaries wrote from the Graham's Town District about a Dutch auction, which is a much simpler affair, but much more profitable, than an English bazaar. " A kind farmer had given a sheep, which was put up for sale by auction, and was speedily knocked down for three guineas— rather a dear sheep; but, dear as it was, it was given back again, so that once more the bidding went on ; and again it was knocked down and given back again ; and so it went on till we realised £40 in less than an hour."

Another fine old veteran in the person of Thomas Hodson, missionary in India for many years went to his rest. " His whole career was one of energy, fidelity, and success." I love to dwell on the memory of these old missionaries. Some of them I knew all my life. Most of them I knew in their prime, and also in the feebleness of old age. And what a reward they have inherited ! " They that turn many to righteousness shall shine as the stars, for ever and ever."

Now, what shall I say at the end of this long retrospect ? I feel that I cannot find words to

say all I would like.   The going through these forty-
five long years of the Society's records has left
with me a memory of events which should not be
forgotten in our history.   It is true it tells a sad
tale of sufferings, of disasters, of " plagues, pesti-
lences, and famines ; of battles, murders, and deaths."
But, at the same time, what a record of gospel
triumphs, of nations almost " born in a day," of
heathens becoming Christians, of man-eaters becoming lovers of their fellows, of kings becoming
" nursing " fathers of the Church, of wandering
tribes settling down to habits of useful labour, and
a thousand other benefits !   Children's homes, hos-
pitals, training institutions, famine-relief works, and
other benevolences, have rescued those ready to
perish.   Education has been scattered far and wide,
with all its advantages.   I may be called an
enthusiast, but I do not hesitate to say that
Wesleyan and other Missions have blessed the
world, in the best sense of the word, more than any
other agency.

I may be forgiven for concluding my Mission
House life by this insertion : " The following
Resolution of the General Committee of the
Wesleyan Missionary Society, on the retirement of
Mr. Thomas Hayes after a service of forty-five
years, was unanimously passed, and directed by the
Committee to be illuminated and presented to him.
It was agreed that, in accepting the recommenda-

tion of the Finance Committee of September 15th relating to the termination of the services of Mr. Thomas Hayes, this Committee places on record its high estimate of his personal character and of the value of his long-continued services. Mr. Hayes has served the Committee faithfully for forty-five years, and the Committee part with him with sincere regret. They assure him of their continued respect and their best wishes for his future health and happiness. It was further determined that a copy of this Resolution be presented to Mr. Hayes in a suitable form.

" *General Treasurers:* J. S. Budgett, J. H. Rigg. *General Secretaries:* J. Kilner, E. Jenkins, M. C. Osborn, G. W. Olver. *Hon. Sec.:* W. Arthur.

" Wesleyan Mission House, London, October 1882."

CHAPTER IX

THE ALLAN LIBRARY

THE splendid collection of books forming this
library was collected by Mr. T. R. Allan,
during many years, and presented by him to the
Conference in the early part of 1884. The donor
was the eldest son of Mr. Thomas Allan, an eminent
solicitor of the city of London, whose office was in
the Old Jewry, and of whom I have a recollection
by his coming to the Mission House to Committees,
and on business connected with the Society. He
was a courtly old gentleman, the *beau ideal* of the
ancient solicitor. I may add here that all the
business he did for Methodism—and that was not a
little—he did gratuitously, and saved the Society
very many pounds. He was a decided Protestant,
and a firm friend of religious liberty. He had
much to do with the improved law of toleration,
passed in 1814.

In the Rev. John Telford's account of " The Allans
of Old Jewry," published in the *Methodist Magazine* in 1887, he says: "It is now time to show
how the library came into Methodist hands. Mr.

Engleburt, who became his clerk in 1839, informs us that, when Mr. Allan returned from his Continental journeys, he sometimes invited his old clerk to come and see him. Among other things, they spoke of the library. Mr. Engleburt knew the expense of warehousing it, and was aware that Mr. Allan had bequeathed it by will to the Wesleyan Conference. He pointed out the large sum that must be paid for legacy duty if it were left by will. 'Why not give it in your own lifetime?' he asked. Mr. Allan thanked him, and promised to consider the suggestion, which had not previously occurred to him.

"At the beginning of 1884 an old gentleman called on Dr. Rigg, at Westminster, with a volume: *A Catalogue of Books, chiefly Theological, collected by T. R. A. In usum Amicorum.* The fly-leaf had the simple inscription: 'T. R. A. begs to present a copy of the Catalogue of his Books to the Rev. Dr. Rigg, 14th January 1884.' Unfortunately, Dr. Rigg was from home. Mr. Allan left no address, so for some time it was a matter of speculation who 'T. R. A.' might be, and what his Catalogue meant. But, at a second visit, the tall feeble old man expressed his intention of presenting his valuable library to the Wesleyan Connexion. In 1884 the library was presented to, and accepted by, the Conference. When Dr. Rigg returned to London, Methodist eyes looked for the first time upon the Methodist library. . . . Some weeks later, treasure after treasure was turned out of the boxes, where they had been jealously and safely guarded. Mr. Hayes was fortunately at liberty, after his long service at the Mission, to arrange the volumes."

It was early in 1884 that the Rev. Theophilus Woolmer asked me if I could take charge of the books named in the foregoing, which had been conveyed to the Book Room. At that moment they were in course of unpacking, which I need not say tried the strength of the Book Room packers, who did the work with a will. Shelving had been, without loss of time, placed round the room, which was formerly the old Conference Office Committee Room, with the addition of two smaller rooms at the end.

As the cases were opened, one after another, and their contents spread out, I seemed to be in a new world. I had always been a lover of books, and here were books to be loved. What treasures of printing—the work of our *first* printers—met one's gaze!—books to be hugged and almost kissed. I did hug some of them, but did not kiss them. In all my life I never handled such treasures. Think of holding in one's hand a folio of 1455, printed five years after the invention of what may almost be termed the divine art of printing. Also books with the original chains by which they were attached to the desks of the churches, monasteries, convents, etc.

I feel that I cannot do better than insert a communication I sent to the *Wesleyan Methodist*

Church Record, which gives a brief sketch of the library's chief treasures. I headed it—

TRAVELS ROUND THE ALLAN LIBRARY

We begin our journey at the large glass-case, known, we daresay, to many who have visited the library. Perhaps the most attractive features are the two Latin Bibles, written respectively 500 and 600 years ago. They are on vellum—in one instance almost as thin as tissue paper—and are fine specimens of caligraphy.

The production of such MSS. by the monks of old must have entailed a vast amount of labour and self-denial, for I have read in occasional glimpses of monkish life that silence, for obvious reasons, was strictly enjoined; in some cases one would be the reader and another the writer, and in other instances copies would be made from a manuscript laid before the copyist. I take it that the ruling motive would be that the work would be put to the credit of the writer in the "great book"—a superstition I cannot find much fault with. Anyhow, the good brothers must have had for the most part a time of quiet peacefulness. I love to dwell on the monastic life of old, so different from the fast rate at which we in the later centuries live. I wish the good monks who copied those old books had written their names at the end of their work, so that one might have known a little about them, if it were but their names.

In the same glass-case—for it is divided into

four sections—we have a Hebrew Scripture, the Prophets and the Hagiographa, dated A.D. 1136 (this is a grand specimen of pen-work); also an Ethiopic MS. containing Isaiah and the Books of Solomon, about 500 years old. There is a fine printed copy of the treatise said to be written by Henry VIII. against Martin Luther, in defence of the Seven Sacraments, for which the Pope sent him the title of Defender of the Faith—a title still retained by our sovereigns, as the letters " F. D." on our coins testify. Alongside of it is Luther's trenchant reply; the first-named is in royal binding, very choice, with a case in which to keep it. Here, too, are some rare early American books on Church government in New England, with accounts of the troubles with the American Indians. Here, too, are some choice specimens of printing, and some quaint ones also: for instance, in the title of one of the books, one line ends with " ma " while the next line begins " de " for the word "made." A fine copy of Coverdale's New Testament, reproduced from the original by photo-zincography, enables us to see how well our early Bible-producers did their work: all honour to them. In this glass-case are to be found still further treasures of Wesleyan interest, including a letter written by John Wesley, addressed to Mrs. Pawson, given by Mr. Smith, of Whitchurch; and John Wesley's surplice, kept for his use at Bath, presented by Mrs. Wiseman. There is also a copy of the smallest edition of

Wesley's Hymns, dated 1815. We have also here a tiny Cicero, which belonged to Dr. Bunting; Dr. A. Clarke's Greek "Elzevir" with his MS. notes, and another Greek Testament with the Doctor's notes, given by Dr. Dallinger; and a pack of Methodist playing-cards, containing Scripture texts on one side, and the same versified on the other. This section of the glass-case is of great interest to Methodists. The lower part is filled with biography and biblical works.

The noble gift of the Fernley Trustees fills a large case. These are all recent books, and were selected mainly by Dr. Moulton. This gift comprises sets of the "Expositor's Bible," the "Cambridge Bible for Schools and Colleges," the "Story of the Nations," the Fernley and Hibbert Lectures, the last edition of the *Encyclopædia Britannica*, all Dr. Dale's Works, Archdeacon Farrar's, Meyer's *Commentary on the New Testament*, Ellicott's Commentary, Philosophical and Scientific series, "Epochs of Church History," and very many more most desirable works. The B section (the room is divided for convenience into sections) contains a large collection of Church History in choice bindings, a fine library copy of Carlyle's Works, Dr. Parker's "People's Bible," given by Rev. C. H. Kelly, "Men of Action" series, "English Statesmen," the chief Poets, and others. Section C embraces Mr. Pocock's generous gift of fifty pounds' worth of valuable books, with Ruskin's, Liddon's,

Maclaren's, and other popular Works. On the opposite side is the noble gift of the Government of 212 volumes of State Records and Calendars of State Papers, all of great value to such a library. Here are also one hundred books selected from Dr. Punshon's library, by Mrs. Punshon's kindness, and books from other generous donors. Altogether, we have about 2000 recent volumes allowed to be taken out.

Our Bible section contains a choice collection of the sacred Scriptures. Of such literature Mr. Allan made a speciality. We possess the Complutensian, or Ximenes, Polyglot—a noble set of books in six volumes, large folio, in splendid binding. This copy cost the donor £110; a finer copy is scarcely to be found. There are also the first five editions of Erasmus's Greek Testament in folio, dating from 1516 to 1535; also Walton's Polyglot, with Castell's Lexicon; early Latin Bibles—one of 1477, by Koburger. Houbigant's great Hebrew Bible—a fine copy in four volumes. The " Bugge "[1] and the "Treacle "[1] Bible, 1549, too, are among our treasures. A fine copy of Dr. Blayney's Oxford Bible, long considered the standard for correctness, but now proved to be far otherwise. The Nuremberg Bible of 1483 is a remarkable work, with its magnificent typography and its quaint illustrations. This is

[1] The " Bugge " Bible is so called from the verse in Psalm xci., being rendered thus : "Thou shalt not be afraid of the bugges by night," etc. The " Treacle " Bible says, "Is there no treacle in Gilead," etc.

described on page **155**.   One feature of this
section, and indeed of all the books in the room,
is the splendid condition of the books.   Mr. Allan
must have paid hundreds of pounds to his binder,
one of the best in London, named Pratt.   Our
Shakespeare, in two large thick folios, is a perfect
beauty; it was given to us by Mr. Purvis, of
Beckenham.   On the table in front of the Bibles
we have other biblical treasures — copies of the
Alexandrine, the Vatican, the Peschito, etc., with
large 4to editions of Young's *Night Thoughts*, with
Blake's weird illustrations; Milton's Works in three
large volumes—the grandest book issued from the
Bulmer Press in 1794 (I was glad to present
this to the library); a reprint of the *Biblia
Pauperum*, with its singular illustrations—an early
block - book.   Then comes another case full of
Bibles in all tongues.   Here is the first printed
Irish Bible in the native character, in two volumes,
1681–85, also an early Manx Bible.   The first
edition of the Syriac New Testament, 1585; also
a set of the Scriptures, translated and printed by
the noble band of Baptist missionaries at Seram-
pore many years ago.   We also have a set of the
Methodist Magazine portraits, from its beginning
in 1778 to 1876, beautifully inlaid by the late Rev.
J. P. Johnson, for Dr. Jobson; these were the gift
of Mrs. Jobson, and are an interesting feature in
this library.   Mr. Whitehead, of Guernsey, gave us
a few years ago a fine set, in a dozen 4to volumes,

of the Survey of Western Palestine—very valuable. Then we have a section for early Wesley items and other Methodist books, including sets of the Connexional Reports, presented by Mr. S. D. Waddy. Another section embraces a large collection of Church History, including several lists of books prohibited by the Popes. A set of the *Arminian* and *Methodist Magazines,* the gift of the late Mrs. W. M. Bunting, is of great service to us ; the later volumes have been added. Another section is devoted to a large collection of Philology, another to Bibliography, another to Missionary Works, another to Scotch Church History, including a set of the Acts of the General Assembly from 1638. The "Fathers" are well represented in grand folio editions, in capital condition of binding. The *Annual Register* from its beginning is a valuable work—in fact, no library is complete without it ; ours is in fine full-calf binding. Sections R, S, T comprise largely the library of the late Dr. Rule, so well known as a biblical scholar, whose books were purchased by Mr. Buller, of Croydon, and presented to this library. Sets of *The Watchman* and *Methodist Recorder,* the gift of Mr. S. D. Waddy, are a valuable and useful addition.

The last stage of our travels to be named is the large table in the centre of the room, on which are laid some choice books, including two dated respectively 1480 and 1481 : these have attached to them the original chains with which they were secured to the reading-desks or libraries in the days of old. There are also sermons by "Jacob the Carthusian," dated 1455—but five years after Gutenberg invented typography, for I believe it is to him that we are indebted for the art. Also is here the *Speculum Passionis,* dated 1507, with its quaint illustrations; here, too, is a magnificent specimen of printing with letters more than half an inch high, the *Psalterium Davidis en Hymnis,* 1521, the grandest bit of printing we possess. Most of the books on this table are in the original wooden boards. In the librarian's room is a choice collection of original Luther tracts, some beautifully bound for Mr. Allan. Our rare engraved portraits of Wesley and others will well repay a visit from anyone curious in such matters.

Among our Methodist treasures were John Nelson's Saddle-Bags, of which I sent an account to the *Methodist Recorder.* I cannot do better than reprint it.

JOHN NELSON'S SADDLE-BAGS

The Allan Library has just been presented with the veritable Saddle-Bags of John Nelson, who, it is well known, was one of the early preachers, labouring incessantly from 1747 to 1774. This interesting gift was made by Sister Banks, of the East End Mission, and was accompanied by the following communication :—

John Nelson's Saddle-Bags were for a long time in the

possession of the late Rev. Matthew Banks, former missionary in the West Indies, whose character and spiritual life were moulded under the leadership of John Nelson the *second*. At the death of Mr. Banks this relic of old Methodism came into the possession of his daughter, E. Jeanie Banks, who now presents them to the Allan Library. Amid labours, privations, and hardships these bags were John Nelson's constant companions; they carried his papers by day, and often formed his only pillow by night.

Few men went through such hardships as did this brave soldier of the Cross; his Journal is a Methodist classic, and will be read by generations to come. It is a book that charmed us in boyhood, and is still read with pleasure and interest. The present generation little knows the price that was paid to secure to us the privileges we enjoy. In those early days many magistrates, clergy, and other officials leagued together to drive out the hated " Methodises," as they were called. Books and pamphlets were written against them that no decent publisher would dare to issue now. Truly, " Other men laboured, and we have entered into their labours." Let us, as Methodists, see to it that we prove ourselves the worthy successors of those who fought such a " good fight."

The mention of this indispensable article of travel carries us back a long way. Travelling then was a toilsome affair, chiefly on horseback, wearying alike to the horse and to the rider. If the latter was a man of bulk and the saddle-bags well lined with books and clothing, it must have been tiring work for poor " Dobbin." The old travelling preachers became much attached to their horses, and many a conversation, we doubt not, took place between them (of course, by the biped) to beguile the weary way. The saddle-bags were the medium through which the Methodist literature of those days was conveyed to the distant parts of the kingdom. What a contrast to the present time, when about thirty tons of books and magazines are sent away by the Book Room every month!

Once we were visited at the library by the Rev. J. H. Merritt, of Denver, Colorado. He was an American, of noble and venerable bearing. On showing him some of the rarities of the library,— among others the " Bugge " Bible, which is also the " Treacle " Bible, and was translated by John Rogers (in the name of Mathewe), the first martyr under Queen Mary,—he told me that his mother was the sixteenth in descent from that noble martyr. I need not say how my heart warmed towards our good American visitor, and a little talk followed. As he had been in England but a week, and had seen few or none of our sights, as a matter of course he had not seen Smithfield, the burning-place of our martyrs; I gave him directions where to find the spot, which from one of the illustrations in Foxe's *Book of Martyrs* showed just where the burning took place, opposite to the gateway of St. Bartholomew's Church, further identified in late years by burnt wood, etc., having been found during digging.

The next day but one our worthy friend Mr. G. W. Munt, of Crouch End, called to consult Foxe's *Book of Martyrs*, of which we have Seymour's valuable edition in eight thick octavo volumes, and are in very fine binding. Mr. Munt wanted information respecting an ancestor who, with his wife and her daughter, gave up their lives for the truth at Colchester in 1557. Several references were found respecting the family of William Munt (or Mount).

The first mention by Foxe is in an "Indenture," wherein William Munt, Alice Munt, and Rose Allin, the daughter of Alice Munt by a former husband, all of Much Bentley, in the county of Essex, are "indicted of heresy"; and that "on the seventh of March, 1557; by 2 o'clock in the morning, one Master Tyrrell took with him the bailiff and two constables with divers others a great number, and besetting the house of the said William Munt round about, called to them at length to open the door, which being done Master Tyrrell with certain of the company went into the chamber where the said Father Mount and his wife lay, willing them to rise, 'for' said he, 'you must go with us to Colchester Castle.' Mother Mount, hearing that, being very sick, desired that her daughter might first fetch her some drink. . . . So her daughter the fore-named Rose Allin, maid, took a stone pot in one hand and a candle in the other, and went to draw drink for her mother; and as she came back again through the house Tyrrell met her, and willed her to give her father and mother good counsel, and advertise them to be better catholic people." Then followed a conversation between the noble girl and her brutal persecutor, which ended by his holding the lighted candle under her hand " till the very sinews cracked asunder." He then thrust her violently from him, using such expressions as cannot be here put on record, but which honest John Foxe does not shrink from giving. He adds : " But she, quietly suffering his rage for the time, at last said, ' Sir, have ye done what ye will do ? ' And he said, ' Yea, and if thou think it be not well, then mend it.' ' Mend it !' said Rose, ' nay, the Lord mend you, and give you repentance, if it be His will. And now, if you think it good, begin at the feet, and burn to the head also. For he that set you at work shall pay you your wages one day, I warrant you.' And so she went and carried her mother drink, as she was commanded."

The ending of this tragedy is thus recorded by Foxe : " In like manner, the same day in the afternoon, were brought forth into the Castle yard, to a place appointed for the same, William Mount, John Johnson, Alice Mount, and Rose Allin aforesaid, which godly, constant persons, after they had made their prayers and were joyfully tied to the stakes, calling upon the name of God, and exhorting the people earnestly to flee from idolatry, suffered their martyrdom with such triumph and joy that the people did no less shout thereat to see it, than at the others that were burnt the same day in the morning." Comment on such suffering, and on a Church which permitted such atrocities, is not needed.

A REMARKABLE BIBLE

In the Allan Library there is one of the most remarkable Bibles in existence. It is dated 1483, is printed in German, and is a very thick folio. Competent authority says it is the most splendid of all the German Bibles, and that it was the first Bible printed at Nuremberg. The paper, characters, press-work, and everything else belonging to Koburger's Bible, prove it to be a masterpiece of typographical excellence. A noteworthy feature is that it has more than sixty bits of leather attached to the leaves, to denote where the illuminations of the larger capitals are to be found. These ornamentations, however, are wanting, never having been executed, save one at the beginning as a specimen. The late Rev. T. Hartwell Horne, no mean judge of typographical excellence, said that it was the printer's *chèf d'œuvre.*

The curious coloured engravings are an interesting study in themselves, and they display the very primitive simplicity of the period when they were executed. To describe the whole would require far more space than I have at my disposal, but a brief account of a few of the more noteworthy will serve to indicate the character of the rest. To begin at the beginning: the first picture represents the creation of Eve, and shows the figure of a lady, with bright yellow tresses reaching half-way down her body, being drawn out of Adam's body while he sleeps upon the grass. The Garden of Eden is surrounded by a well-built wall, and has a church in it. Another picture shows Cain and Abel offering their sacrifices. They wear leggings and pointed stockings, and for an altar have a table with turned legs. In the picture of the Deluge we have a flat-bottomed square built barge, with a deck and handrail, and on the deck a barn-like building surmounted by a pigeon-house. An ape and a peacock are perched on the handrail, and Noah (with his name over him) looks out of a window, watching for the return of the dove.

I believe it is the opinion of most scholars that the Jews conceived the angels to be males, but our artist here, like most of those of to-day, always represents them as females, though the text speaks of men. Three lady angels occupy Jacob's ladder, there being no room for more. It is probable that at the period when this Bible was printed there was but little accurate knowledge of the manners and customs of the East, and the artists were thus compelled to depict the architecture and the dress of their own countries and times. Hence in the burial of Jacob we see a substantial coffin, bearing his name, about to be placed in a grave the headstone of which bears the names of Abraham and Isaac, a hill in the background being crowned by a mediæval castle ; while at the burial of Aaron the mourners are assisted by a monk. Again, in the battle against the Amalek the hands of Moses are held up by two warriors wearing the dress of the fourteenth century, and the bearers of the ark in the walk round Jericho wear the armour and carry the arms of the same period. The royal Psalmist is also represented as wearing a large hat made of fur ; while three dogs—one a French poodle—disport themselves in a cosy room with a settee in it. Turning to the New Testament, I may mention that, in the genealogy recorded by St. Matthew, the supposed owners of the names are standing in front of the writer in the strangest of attire. The Evangelist sits in a straight-backed chair at a writing-desk, with a large-winged angel standing alongside. St. Mark is writing his Gospel, with the Resurrection taking place before him, with the strange blunder of the soldiers asleep around the tomb. St. Luke, with spectacles on, is recording his narrative ; while St. John sits in a cauldron of oil over a well-lit furnace. One attendant is ladling the boiling liquid over his head and shoulders. Then, again, he is represented in Patmos, a small space of ground of a few feet in extent, surrounded by water. He sits with a modern-shaped book on his knees and an ink-horn in his hand. Death, on the pale horse, is a horrid skeleton with a large scythe. The seven-headed beast is a strange compound; the dragon, painted yellow, is on his hind-legs, holding an argument with his auditors. The bad lady of Babylon is dressed in fifteenth-century costume, with lofty head-dress. In another picture hell is shown as an enormous dragon's mouth, into which popes, cardinals, bishops, kings, etc., are being driven.

Such were the methods used to teach Scripture knowledge in ancient times. This old Bible, with its quaint illustrations, is a real study.

Other incidents of an interesting nature in connection with the Allan Library might be named, but these must suffice. It only remains for me to add that, feeling I was getting into years, and had not the strength I formerly possessed, and having been more than sixty years in active employment, I felt the time had come for me to retire, and I asked that I might be released from my duties. The Committee accepted my resignation, and my worthy chief, the Rev. Nehemiah Curnock, kindly inserted the following paragraph in the *Methodist Recorder*. It was far too flattering.

" Mr. Thomas Hayes is about to retire from the service of the Book Room and Allan Library, after many years of close and valuable work. Mr. Hayes is seventy-seven years of age. He was employed from a boy for a long time at the Mission House, and retired on a pension. He has been the assiduous librarian at City Road for some years. His knowledge of Wesleyan Missions and relics is unique; and as a referee on matters concerning the Wesley family and early Methodism he has been most useful. His retirement is quite his own doing. He feels that with old age, deafness, and the desire for quiet and rest before he passes on, it is well that he should now take a Sabbath at the end of earthly toil. He has done a good work, and those who know him wish him peace and joy, and the Divine blessing."

CHAPTER X

A FEW years ago Mr. Westerdale successfully carried out his large scheme of putting City Road Chapel and Wesley's House into complete repair. For the success of this effort much credit was due to the Trustees of the Wilson Street estate, for so generously handing over to the City Road Trustees the large sum of £5000, which they had received from the Great Eastern Railway Company for their little piece of freehold land, which cost them originally £500. This now forms part of the site of their large terminus in Bishopsgate Street. This grand gift, with other generous contributions from friends, was the means of finishing a work that had long been needed. As a matter of course, Wesley's House was to share in the blessing; and, although the whole business was an expensive undertaking, it was a success, and a credit to all concerned. The house is probably about one hundred and twenty years old, and no doubt was built as soon as could be after the chapel was finished. In all likelihood it will last as long again.

As I am not writing a history of City Road Chapel, I must refer my readers who want to know more of our "Cathedral" to Stevenson's *History*, a book replete with Methodist lore of the surrounding neighbourhood.

It was at Mr. Westerdale's request that I arranged in part the Wesley items in the house. The floor containing Mr. Wesley's rooms has now an interesting and increasing collection of Wesley relics, contributed by loving friends, of more or less interest. There is a beautiful case of Wedgwood medallions of Wesley; they are perfect gems, and were generously given by Mr. R. T. Smith, of Whitchurch. The room also contains Hone's large three-quarter-length portrait of Wesley; also a life-size head and shoulders painting of Dr. Coke; with several fine old engraved portraits of Wesley, with three large glazed frames of the chief incidents in our Founder's life. The teapot must not be forgotten. It is of family proportions, and is carefully preserved. I was told that a rich American offered a fabulous amount for it.

On a former page I have given my humble opinion as to Wesley's death-chamber, about which there is uncertainty. The little, very little room at the back of the house, known as Wesley's praying room, I will say nothing about, it is too sacred, preferring to leave the good man there alone with his God.

One may easily imagine that in the early days

of the chapel there was much vacant ground round about it. Of course the Bunhill Fields Cemetery was there, in which so much "bonnie dust" lies buried. What a Valhalla of the great and the good it is! There is also the Artillery Company's practising ground. In the very olden times of Agincourt and Crecy the London archers were a force to be reckoned with. They practised the bow and arrow and cross-bow manœuvres with such precision that the steel-pointed bolts fell with telling effect on the enemy. The neighbourhood is of historic interest, and was just outside the city walls. The site of the old wall is represented by the street known as "London Wall" at the present day. The old city has a charm for me, which I cannot help feeling; though to speak of the warlike doings of our ancestors is a digression, after writing about that pre-eminent man of peace and love, John Wesley.

The first time I walked up the stairs of Wesley's house, I thought of the good old man treading the same stairs, and holding on to the balustrade, or using a walking-stick. Then in imagination I saw him seated in the front room in the old arm-chair (one of the relics of those early days left behind),— if in cold weather, near the fire; then I imagine I see little Jemmy Rogers (of whom I have before spoken), creeping to the dear old man's side, to be drawn to his knees, and pleasantly chatted with, for Mr. Wesley was a lover of children as well as of everybody. Mr. and Mrs. Hester Ann Rogers lived in the house and looked after the old patriarch. I daresay many a passer-by turned to look at Mr. Wesley's venerable form as he went into the house. By this time he had become a well-known figure. How one's mind might run away into these imaginary, but quite probable, scenes.

I wish there had been more of Mr. Wesley's furniture left: for instance, what an object of interest would have been the bedstead or chair on which he died! The fine old staircase clock is still there, a thorough " grandfather's clock." The beautiful old bureau is a fine bit of old cabinet work of probably one hundred and fifty years ago. How the writers of Methodist local history love to dwell on the Wesley relics in all parts of the country! The chairs on which he sat, the stones on which he stood to preach, even the cup he used when somebody's great-grandmother entertained him, have been carefully preserved or noted. I, too, am somewhat of a relic-worshipper—at least of Wesley relics.

HACKNEY ROAD CHAPEL AND SUNDAY SCHOOL

is but a step of about half a mile from City Road Chapel, and a few words about this loved sanctuary must be said. In 1838 I joined the Sunday school, and the following year began to meet in class. About a dozen lads joined the Society at

that time. I had the advantage of one of the
best of Sunday-school teachers, Mr. John Williams.
The earnest appeals of our teachers and of the
Superintendent, Mr. John Jackson, and of the
Secretary, Mr. James Stephens, had a good effect
on many of the youngsters. The school then ran
along the back of the old Middlesex Chapel, on the
site of which the chapel now stands. I remember
the stone-laying, when Mr. T. Farmer, the "master
mason" of his day, officiated. In a sketch of the
Jubilee of the Sunday school, written by Mr. C. W.
Brabner some years ago, there is a large collection
of interesting facts connected with the school. I
love to dwell on the memories of our chapel, they
are so pleasant. I often think of good old Mr. W.
W. Williams (father of Mr. Lisle Williams), and
his magnificent voice for singing, the remembrance
of which has often been a benediction to me since.
Then there was good John Vanner, to whom the
chapel was much indebted for material help and
wise counsel. His sons are an honour to an
honoured father. Mr. Engleburt, Mr. T. Early,
and others I love to think upon.

Of the Rev. Samuel Wilkes' work at Hackney
Road too much cannot be said. He came to us
when we were "brought very low," all our well-to-
do families having gone away to do work for the
Master in suburban places. His earnest devotion
to his work was followed by a much better state of
things. He gathered round him a noble band of

workers, and established many agencies, making it comparatively easy for his successors to carry on the good work. The late Dr. Moulton said that he considered Mr. Wilkes' work at Hackney Road one of the bravest efforts of any Methodist preacher, and he held him in very high esteem. Had Mr. Wilkes' physical strength been equal to the strain, it was the intention of the Rev. J. Ernest Clapham, Home Mission Secretary, to have asked the Conference for his reappointment. We shall not soon forget him at Hackney Road. He fills a large place in my heart. The Rev. Samuel Chadwick succeeded Mr. Wilkes. His year's stay was all too short.

Needless to say, I formed many friendships in the Sunday school. What a succession of worthy men and women who taught for Jesus pass through my memory! Two of the superintendents occupied much of my regard — Mr. John W. Brabner, and his brother Mr. C. W. Brabner. Mr. John died suddenly some years ago; his brother still survives, full of good works. Mr. William Page, the present able Superintendent of the Sunday school, I know would not thank me for saying all I should like about him, so I will be silent, though reluctantly. The last twenty-five years of my Sunday - school life was as its librarian.

CHAPTER XI

THE CONFERENCE OFFICE

MY connection with the Allan Library naturally brought me much into contact with the Conference Office, both being at first under the same roof. Frequently, in my boyhood, Mission House business took me there, since which time I have seen a long succession of Book Stewards, managers, heads of departments, clerks, and warehousemen.

The Book Room has an interesting history, and the following communication which I sent to the *Methodist Recorder* a while ago it is hoped may not be unacceptable to my readers.

" SOLD AT THE FOUNDERY "

The first mention of the Foundery as a place where Mr. Wesley's publications were to be had was in 1740 on the title‑page of *Hymns and Sacred Poems* of that date, and this may be regarded as the origin of the Methodist Book Room. The history of the Foundery is too well known to Methodists to need repeating here. The late Mr.

Stevenson, in his *History of City Road Chapel*, to which I am indebted for some of these jottings, says that it was situated on the boundary of Moorfields, in a by-path called Windmill Hill. I may add that it was on the east side of the present Tabernacle Street, near the corner of Worship Street. Mr. Wesley's first bookseller was James Hutton, the Moravian, whose shop was in the Strand, just through the old Temple Bar; but it was at Mr. Bray's house in Little Britain that the unsold books were stored, till the Foundery was taken, repaired, and made ready for occupation, the end of the band-room being fitted up with shelves. Here for forty years Mr. Wesley carried on what soon became an extensive book-trade. Thomas Butts and William Briggs were the first book agents. They were succeeded by Samuel Francks, of whom Charles Wesley speaks well in his Journal, both as a man of business and as a Christian. Sad to say, "poor Francks," as John Wesley calls him, yielded to the pressure of disease, and hanged himself in the Foundery in 1773. Strangely enough, a fortnight afterwards, Matthews, the Foundery schoolmaster, followed his sad example. What a gruesome business!

John Atlay was the first Book Steward appointed by Mr. Wesley. His business qualifications, however, did not commend him. He told Mr. Wesley that his stock of books in London was worth more than £13,000, but in reality it was not of more value than £5000, as estimated by two booksellers employed by Mr. Wesley to ascertain the worth. He was in office for five years; George Whitfield followed from 1779 till 1804; Robert Lomas from 1804 till 1808; Thomas Blanshard from 1808 till 1823; and John Kershaw from 1823 till 1827.

Mr. Mason, whose praise cannot be sufficiently set forth, and who may be regarded as the saviour of the Book Room from its financial difficulties, occupied the stewardship for nearly thirty-seven years—from 1827 to 1864; he attended to his duties to within half an hour of his death. He was succeeded by the late Dr. Jobson, who died in 1881.

In 1777, when City Road Chapel was built, the book-selling was removed thither to the house adjoining the Morning Chapel, which was afterwards the residence of Mr. Benson. The packing-room and warehouse for storage of the books was under the Morning Chapel. What a contrast between such a dungeon and the present noble warehouse!

In 1808 No. 14 City Road was taken, with premises in the rear, largely increasing the space occupied. It was in 1839, the Centenary year, that the most extensive alterations and additions were made. In 1882 the house now occupied as the Saloon was taken, the windows of which form one of the sights of City Road. In 1889 the lease of the three or four houses extending to Castle

Street was secured, mainly for the erection of the building containing the Allan Library.

The Book Room has been largely benefited by a succession of good business men as Book Stewards and managers. Packing-time, at the end of each month, is a sight worth seeing. The warehouse is a perfect beehive, and the mass of books, magazines, etc., sent away every month, is enormous. It fills one with surprise, while going through the premises, to see the mass of paper and books stored up in the rooms. Few publishing houses can report such a successful career.

I need not apologise for inserting what Mr. Tyerman wrote in his *Life and Times of John Wesley* about the Foundery.

" The entire cost of the old Foundery was about £800. This was the first Methodist meeting-house of which the metropolis could boast, and a brief description of it may not be out of place. It stood in the locality called ' Windmill-hill,' now known by the name of Windmill Street, a street that runs parallel with City Road, and abuts on the north-west corner of Finsbury Square. The building was placed on the east side of the street, some sixteen or eighteen yards from Providence Row; and measured about forty yards in front from north to south, and about thirty-three yards in depth from east to west. There were two front doors—one leading to the chapel, and the other to the preacher's house, school, and band-room. A bell was hung in a plain belfry, and was rung every morning at five o'clock for early service, and every evening at nine for family worship, as well as at sundry other times. The chapel, which would accommodate some 1500 people, was without pews; but on the ground floor, immediately before the pulpit, about a dozen seats with back rails, appropriated to female worshippers. Under the front gallery were the free seats for women, and under the side galleries the free seats for men. The front gallery was used exclusively by females, and the side galleries by males. 'From the beginning,' says Wesley, 'the men and women sat apart, as they always did in the primitive church; and none were suffered to call any place their own, but the first comers sat down first. They had no pews, and all the benches for rich and poor were of the same construction.' The band-room was behind the chapel, on the ground floor, some eighty feet long and twenty feet wide, and accommodated about 300 persons. Here the classes met; here, in winter, the five o'clock morning service was conducted; and here was held, at two o'clock on Wednesdays and Fridays, weekly meetings for prayer and intercession. The north end of the room was used for a school, and was fitted up with desks; and at the south end was 'the book-room' for the sale of Wesley's publications. Over the band-room were apartments for Wesley, in which his mother died; and at the end of the chapel was a dwelling-house for his domestics and assistant preachers; while attached to the whole was a building used as a coach-house and stable.

" This was really the cradle of London Methodism. Here Wesley began to preach at the end of 1739. The character of the services held in this rotten, pantile-covered building, may be learned from Wesley's Works. Wesley began the service with a short prayer, then sang a hymn, and preached usually half an hour, then sang a few verses of another hymn, and concluded with a prayer. His constant theme was: salvation by faith, preceded by repentance, and followed by holiness. The place was rough, and the people poor; but the service simple, scriptural, beautiful. No wonder that such a priest, shut out of the elaborately wrought pulpits of the Established Church, and now cooped up within a pulpit made of 'rough deal boards,' should be powerful, popular, and triumphant."

One feature of the Conference Office is its un-equalled collection of Wesley letters and manu-scripts, which have been in possession of the authorities for a long time. Many of them were purchased from the family of the Rev. Charles Wesley, our poet, and included a number of volumes of MSS. hymns in his beautiful hand-writing. These, with other choice items, are in a large iron safe in the Book Steward's office. Needless to say that Mr. Kelly guards them with the greatest care, and they are shown only by himself to specially favoured visitors.

It has been a pleasurable task to me to put many of the precious items into repair, which was needed. When I first handled Mr. Wesley's "Deed of Declaration," enrolled in Chancery in 1784, I was quite excited, and felt something like a thrill when I realised that I was holding in my hands the Magna Charta of Methodism, the sheet-anchor by which the Connexion is held together. The deed is in three large sheets of vellum, signed at the end by John Wesley. It contains the names of one hundred of the preachers forming the Conference to carry on the work of Methodism at the Founder's death Of course it is the original deed, and not a copy. It is preserved in a beautiful morocco case, and kept in a large iron safe. There are many important documents also in the safe, such as Charles Wesley's marriage settlement with Miss Gwynne, in which John Wesley guarantees the sum of one hundred per annum for his brother. But the Poll Deed (for importance) swallows up all the rest. No place could be too safe for such a document. In 1884 the centenary of the enrolling of the Deed was celebrated at City Road Chapel, when Dr. Osborn gave a most interesting account of the transaction. It is true the large iron safe in the Book Steward's room is crowded with treasures, but many of our most important documents and relics have never been there, but are deposited in the Iron Strong Room and its interior safe.

I early had a love for old letters, especially those written by the venerable Wesley; and it was a real delight to put such into good condition, mounting them in suitable books, and I think now with pleasure of the part I took in such loving work.

A year or two ago a discovery was made of a large mass of Wesley and other manuscripts at the Book Room. These important documents were entrusted to me for repair and mounting.

Dr. Jobson rendered a great service to the Book Room, nay, to all Methodism, by causing a large mass of Wesley papers, which had accumulated, to be properly repaired and inlaid in large folio volumes. It was done by the late Rev. J. P. Johnson, quite an artist in that kind of work, from whom I gained much knowledge. Among the treasures in the large safe are printed copies of the first Minutes, 1744 to 1747—printed, strange to say, at Dublin in 1749. Also the first edition of the *Rules of the United Societies*, 1743. There were three editions of this date, issued in London, Bristol, and Newcastle.

The Conference Office library is a very valuable one, and contains the best and largest collection of books on Methodism and by Methodist writers. Biography forms a large section, also Mission Histories. Most of the Connexional Reports are to be found there, with bound volumes of the various Methodist newspapers. Fine sets of the Arminian and Methodist Magazines from their beginning, also sets of the Minutes of Conferences from 1744, with all the Book Room serials in bound volumes. The most valuable portion of the library is the collection of early editions of the Wesley prose and poetical books and tracts; in some cases there are every edition that was published. For many, very many years, a copy of every book published by the Book Room has been placed on the shelves.

It would be interesting to give here a sketch of the old Conference Office, say early last century, when the printing was done there. I remember seeing a relic of this department in the person of good old Thomas Cordeux, with his knee-breeches and shoe-buckles, a little spare old man, whose name will be found on very many of the old books printed at the office. In course of time the printing there was given up, and the work done by the trade. Some of the best printed books are now issued by the Conference Office.

It was for some time on my mind to make a catalogue of the Conference Office library, and with permission I undertook the task. It was a long job, but, as it was a voluntary one, I felt the more interest in it. I arranged the books on my own plan, which I have every reason to believe gave satisfaction to the Book Steward and Committee. This was the closing part of my work at the Book Room, for I asked permission to retire soon after. The Book Committee kindly passed the following resolution :—

" On the motion of the Rev. N. Curnock, seconded by the Rev. W. L. Watkinson, the Book Committee on Monday passed a resolution on the retirement of Mr. Thomas Hayes, late Assistant at the Allan Library, expressive of its high appreciation of his character, devotion to his work, loyalty to Methodism, and rare attainments as an authority on Methodist literature and Wesley relics. Mr. Hayes is seventy-seven years of age, and has been in Methodist employment nearly all his life; having gone as a mere boy to the first Mission House in Hatton Garden; and only left the Book Room within the last few days."

CHAPTER XII

JOTTINGS OF A METHODIST BOOK-WORM AND ANTIQUARIAN

IT was, I think, in the first week of my going to the Wesleyan Mission House in 1837, as office-boy, that I spent my first twopence for a book. I look back with horror to think that that one book has grown to *ten thousand*, with which my small house at Dalston is now crammed. Though much discomfort arises from having so many books, yet the pleasures enjoyed in rummaging the bookstalls—for these have been my chief resorts—are very many, and known only to such collectors. Now and then a prize has rewarded me for my labour, and I have gone on my way rejoicing.

Every bookstall searcher is bound to meet with rarities now and then; it would be strange if he did not. Even now, as I look back on my early collecting days, I feel a pleasure as I call to mind such instances of success. I have stood at the bookstalls overhauling the books till my fingers were all but frozen by the cold, so great was my passion for "old books," as they are often very disrespectfully called. Seldom a day passed in my earlier life without a purchase. In addition to the opportunity thus afforded of meeting now and then with a rarity, there is the pleasure of expectation that the next book will be something choice.

I have met with black-letter books, old stamped vellum books, books in wooden boards, old Bibles of from two hundred to three hundred years old. One purchase for a few pence must be nameless, beyond saying that it is called "An Effectual Shove," etc. It is but a tract in a small volume of other pieces of divinity, a good rousing sermon, but with an outrageous title. But times have changed, and, as in the case of most hobbies, the desire has passed away. I know of persons who at one time were as eager for such things as they are now eager*less*.

The auction rooms, too, were fruitful in such findings. On one occasion I heard that some early Wesley books were to be sold; the sale was to be the next day, so I went the same evening to look through the lots, and saw some very choice items. So struck was I with their rarity that I got very little sleep that night, fearing lest someone else should also know their value and run up the prices too high. However, at the sale I had them at my own price, and came home very well satisfied with that evening's purchase.

By a strange coincidence a few years ago the libraries of some half-dozen great Methodist collectors, who all died within twelve months or so of each other, were disposed of by auction, and I secured many choice books. It seldom occurs that such a mass of desirable books is brought to the hammer at one time. At one of these sales a copy of the Charlestown Hymn-book, prepared by John Wesley in 1737, originally bought for ten shillings, was run up to twenty-three pounds.

I owe much of my acquaintance with books to my dear old friend, the Rev. W. B. Boyce, whose clerk I was at the Mission House. He was a great book-buyer, and was so kind and thoughtful that he would and *could* give information on almost any subject named to him. There were few persons also who had such a knowledge of early Methodist books as Dr. Osborn, and from him I learned much. Dr. Punshon took me to several of the Conferences to attend to Mission House matters during the sittings, and this gave me an opportunity of rummaging the book-shops of several large towns.

Not that I have confined myself to Methodist books. Being known to many of the bookstall owners, I have had good opportunities of picking up interesting items. Sometimes I have had the key of the store to search through to my heart's content, while the owner was elsewhere selling his books. But, while I have been trusted by some, others would not leave me out of their sight, so suspicious are some people.

An acquaintance with Wesley and Wesleyan letters was also formed in my earlier life. Dr. Hoole, one of our best antiquarians, sent me on one occasion to look at some letters of John Wesley, offered to him by an autograph dealer, who was much shocked when I proved to him that the signature only was Wesley's. He said it made a difference of some pounds to him in their value. When one of the American bishops called on me to look over my items at home, he was rather grieved that I would not sell to him one of my treasures—an interesting letter of John Wesley's which I have framed. A companion to it is the portrait of Mr. Wesley preaching under a tree. This portrait appeared in the "Notes on the Old Testament," and has in Wesley's writing the date of his birth; an interesting item. The arranging and mounting of the Wesley and other early rarities in the Mission House museum, and also in the Allan Library, was to me quite a labour of love. The Wesley Centenary Exhibition in 1891, when a collection of relics relating to our venerable Founder was exhibited, such as had never been brought together before, was a happy time to me. It was while showing a gentleman the cases that I found I was speaking with Mr. Lecky, the great historian, who had written very favourably of Wesley and Methodism. He kindly shook my hand.

I am tempted to speak of visits to the collections of the Rev. Richard Green at Didsbury, the Rev. Marmaduke Riggall at Budleigh Salterton, to Mr. Wright of Wolverhampton, and to Mr. George Stampe at Grimsby. This last-named visit comes very vividly to my memory. We sat, after the family had retired, till the small hours of the morning, he as pleased to show his choice collection as I was to see it. We then crept up to our rooms like two burglars, so as not to disturb the household. There are other collections which it has not been my good fortune to inspect; but I must refer at length to one of the best I have seen, namely, the Highfield Collection, formed by R. Thursfield Smith, Esq., J.P., of Whitchurch.

THE HIGHFIELD COLLECTION

During a fortnight's stay at Mr. Smith's hospitable home I was able to make a thorough investigation of the collection. To begin: the busts number thirty-five; the gem of them all is one by Roubilliac, but there are also two by Wedgwood. There are medallion miniatures in blue, black, pale green, one exquisitely modelled by Flaxman, and also one of life-size in bold relief by Mohr. Teapots, jugs, cups and saucers, basins, etc., all bearing our Founder's likeness, are in abundance. Also a volume of choice letters written by John Bennet, John Berridge, William Cowper, John Newton, William Grimshaw, James Hervey, John Nelson, Lady Huntingdon, Lady Darcy Maxwell, Marmaduke Gwynne, Vincent Perronet, Henry Venn, with an interesting document sent to Wesley in 1740, signed by the eminent Moravian P. Molther, James Hutton, senior and junior, and others. There are half a dozen letters written by Whitefield, dated from 1739 to 1767; also one by Hester Ann Roe, afterwards Mrs. Rogers, to Mr. Swindells, of London, urging his acceptance of the Saviour—pleadings which happily were not in vain.

A most precious volume contains about sixty Wesley letters, and includes one written by Mrs. Susannah Wesley, and six by Charles Wesley, the "Poet of Methodism." Mr. Wesley's Journal kept while in Georgia is among the treasures.

The choice collection of hymns written by the Wesleys, in book or tract form, all in first editions, with but one or two exceptions, I must leave to a better expert than I am to describe; I never saw such a set. The larger part of them belonged to the late Mr. Love, an ardent collector, from whose executors they were purchased. Mr. Smith has completed them from his own stores, and put them into beautiful bindings to match. Some of the hymn-tracts are of excessive rarity, and very seldom met with nowadays. If the bibliography of the Highfield Collection could be written, it would make a valuable addition to our literary stores. With many of the volumes there is an interesting history from inscriptions written inside, etc. No doubt, copies of some of these rarities are to be found in Methodist homes, and to know *where* they are would be interesting.

It is a pleasure known only to Methodist autograph collectors to be able to read and handle letters written by good men and women whose names have become "household words" in Methodism. In imagination one seems to be present with the writers, whose letters, to me, form part of their very selves, and I revelled in their contents. These valuable letters have been carefully mounted in good blank books. The large volume of Presidents' letters and portraits is the finest set I have seen. A large mass of the late Rev. Rowland Hill's correspondence with his friends is also a valuable acquisition.

Some time ago a doubt was expressed in the Methodist press as to whether it was at the Land's End that Charles Wesley composed his glorious hymn—"Lo! on a narrow neck of land." I sent the following to the *Recorder* :—

"What a pity to rob *our* Land's End of the credit of being the birthplace of this grand

hymn! If Charles Wesley's manuscript was here
in the Allan Library for five minutes, I think the
true birthplace of the hymn would be settled.
Supposing the hymn to have been written in
America, what an interesting English Methodist
landmark it removes. On a visit to Cornwall
a few years ago, when a party of us went to the
Land's End, our guide was asked where the spot
was on which Charles Wesley composed the
hymn. 'Here,' he exclaimed, 'where I am
now standing,' at the same time striking his
stick on a large flat stone, and he at once quoted
the first verse—

> Lo, on a narrer neck o' lan',
> 'Twixt two onboonded seas I stan',
> So cure and sensible,

and more in the same style, at which we smiled."

The Book Room having determined to bring
out a corrected edition of Wesley's Journals and
Letters, it was taken up by several Methodist
antiquarians, and the *Recorder* kindly inserted the
following :—

"Mr. Thomas Hayes, of the Allan Library, has
also been working for many years on these and
similar subjects. He writes as follows :—' I need
not say with what pleasure I read the announcement that it is intended to devote some space
weekly to Notes and Queries on the Letters and
Journals of John Wesley. I have already gathered
about two hundred letters from the old magazines

and newspapers, and shall have much pleasure in placing them at the service of the Rev. W. L. Watkinson. In Wesley's Works, vols. 12 and 13, 923 letters are printed. From these a choice selection might be made, for I suppose every letter written by our venerable Founder will not be inserted in the volume, or volumes, which I understand the Book Committee has determined to publish. Many original letters have come to light since the Works were published in 1829–31. A printed letter I have illustrates Wesley's ready wit and skill as a letter-writer. One of his preachers wrote to him saying that he wished to resign his position, as he thought he was not in his right place. Mr. Wesley replied: " Dear Brother, you are not in your right place, for you are doubting when you ought to be praying.— Yours, etc." ' "

AN EVENING AMONG " KELMSCOTT " BOOKS

I was indebted to a very worthy friend of mine, Mr. E. Crawshaw, F.R.G.S., of Tollington Park, for a most enjoyable evening spent a while ago at his house, among his " Kelmscott " books, of which he has a choice collection. He possesses some very interesting Wesley items—books, letters, portraits, etc.; but his Kelmscotts are the choicest treasures. Why the books have this name is that they were printed at Kelmscott House, Hammersmith, from types invented by Wm. Morris, poet, printer, and genius. As an inventor in typography he has left his mark on history. Every one of his books sells far above its published price. The inventor's greatest treasure is his edition of Chaucer's Works, published at £20 (the last realised £112), and when a copy is offered at the auction rooms there is much excitement. The type invented by Morris seemed to me to consist of the finest old "black letter" and "Old English," apparently a combination, but it requires a better expert than I am to describe it as it ought to be. Mr. Crawshaw described his "Chaucer" to me as "the finest book ever printed"; and he is no mean judge, for his shelves abound with some of the best specimens of printing I have seen.

The Kelmscott Press was the issue of a long-standing hope. A fellow - student at Oxford was his life-long friend, Mr. Burne-Jones (afterwards made a baronet), with whom he delighted to turn over the pages of the splendid manuscripts in the Bodleian Library. The ideal of the "book beautiful" marked Morris's "Chaucer," for typography, ornament, and illustration combined, as the grandest book that has been issued from the press since the invention of typography; and we realise the indebtedness of our time to William Morris as the originator of a new era in book - making. "A thing of beauty is a joy for ever." Never were these words more applicable than in these books.

One of the London Methodist Guilds gathered in a good number a few years ago at the Allan Library to see its treasures, and to hear me read the following paper I had prepared. I may be pardoned for inserting it :—

A CHAT ABOUT BOOKS

Before the invention of printing a variety of substances were used to communicate certain events. Probably brick and stone were the first used. We read that the Ten Commandments were written on tables of stone. The Egyptian obelisks were records of events, or fulsome panegyrics on the builders themselves or on the gods they worshipped. During recent explorations at Babylon, the ledgers, as we may term the stone cylinders of that ancient race of people, of a banking firm were exhumed and deciphered. They are in the British Museum. Among them were found records of two leases, accompanied by plans of the estates which they concern, executed with all the skill and accuracy of modern conveyancing. The deed is witnessed by So-and-so, the son of the judge; by So-and-so, the son of the builder; by So-and-so, the son of the boat-builder; and by So-and-so, the son of the cup-bearer. None were to repudiate the transaction, under certain penalties. This throws much light on the prophet Jeremiah's purchase of the field of Hananeel.

Lead also was anciently used for preserving

laws, etc. The method of writing or engraving was with a graver, or style of iron. Hesiod's works, we are told, were written on tablets of lead; and an old French traveller tells us that he bought at Rome a book entirely of lead—the leaves, cover, and stick in which the rings were inserted, which held the book together, being all of lead.

Brass, too, was in former use, for we have read that the celebrated Twelve Tables among the Romans were engraved on twelve tablets of brass; and Dr. Buchanan, the Syrian traveller, tells us of six ancient tablets containing privileges, etc., being of this metal. Books with wooden leaves were in use before Homer's time; they were covered with wax, and the writing was executed with sharp-pointed iron pens, not, I imagine, Gillott's patent, but hard unsplit pens. In the Apocrypha (2 Esdras xiv. 24, 37, 44) we read of two hundred and four books being made of boxwood, and written upon by certain "swift" writers. The ancient Britons used to write on smoothed sticks squared. The leaves of trees were also used in ancient times, and down to later periods have been in use in parts of India.

Linen was formerly another substance made use of by the Egyptians; a linen book has been found in a mummy-case now in our great Museum.

Parchment—the skin of sheep or goats after

undergoing certain processes—was much in vogue. Josephus tells us that the copy of the law presented by Ptolemy, King of Egypt, was written on parchment in letters of gold. St. Paul bids Timothy bring the books, but especially the parchments. In ancient writings the skins were glued or sewed together, and rolled up, generally on a cylinder of wood, and called rolls, or vols. (from the Latin word *volvendo*), to roll up. Many references in Scripture there are to this form of ancient books or rolls (Ps. xl. 7; Jer. xxxvi. 2; Ezek. ii. 9). Perhaps the literal rendering of Luke iv. 17 would be, "and *unrolling* the book he found the place where it was written, The Spirit of the Lord is upon me," etc. The most ancient kind of paper was made from the inner part of the papyrus, a sort of rush growing on the banks of the Nile; and from this is derived our word paper.

You have all heard, no doubt, of the famous Alexandrian Library, containing 500,000 rolls or volumes. When Alexandria was captured by the Saracens, under Amri, from the Greeks, A.D. 640, he wrote to the Caliph Omar for instructions as to these books. Said Omar, " If there be nothing in the books contrary to the word of God (the Koran), they are utterly useless; but if they contain anything repugnant to that book, they ought to be destroyed. I command you therefore to destroy them all." We are told that it took months to burn them, for heating the baths, etc.

In olden times monks were the fabricators of books. In most monasteries a room was set apart for the work of translation or copying, called the Scriptorium, provided with forms and desks. The monks were under orders to keep strict silence, so that though their labours were useful, yet how tedious! Some did the illuminating, or ornamentation, of the books. There is in the British Museum a copy of the Bible made by one Alcuin, an English monk, during the years 778 and 800—a space of twenty-two years—for the great Charlemagne. This ancient and highly interesting monument of piety and labour was purchased years ago by the Trustees of the Museum for £750. I have seen it, and it is a sight to feast one's eyes upon. In the same Museum there are many gorgeous specimens of books, mostly of devotion, with the colours of the capitals most brilliant, as though of yesterday's workmanship; inlaid also with gold and precious stones. Skelton, the Poet Laureate, in his *Garland of Laurel*, written about the year 1510, rapturously alludes to the splendid bindings of those old times :—

With that of the books loosened with the clasps,
   The margin was illumined all with golden rails,
And bice, pictured with grasshoppers and wasps,
   With butterflies and fresh peacocks' tails.
It would have made a man whole had he been right sickly,
   To behold how it was garnished and bound,
Encovered with gold of tissue fine,
   The clasps and bullions were worth a thousand pound,
With rubies and carbuncles the borders did shine,
   And with mosaic gold was written each line.

Some of the producers of these books sold them at high prices, as they were executed only for kings, nobles, and church dignitaries. When a book was lent for transcribing, an additional copy was the price of the favour. In a Scotch monastery, I have somewhere read, sixteen volumes formed the library, so scarce were books in olden times.

Scriptures in part, and legends of the saints, mainly formed the subjects of these early libraries; I speak of the English principally. In 1299 the Bishop of Winchester borrowed a Bible in two folio volumes, but gave a bond drawn up with great solemnity. When this Bible was given to the convent, with one hundred marks in money, the monks founded a daily mass for the soul of the donor. Before the year 1300 the library of Oxford College consisted of a few tracts only, kept in chests. In those early times, a French countess paid two hundred sheep, five quarters of wheat, and the same quantity of rye and millet, for a copy of a certain bishop's book of homilies.

But what a mighty change came when the noble art of printing was invented! Surely, if the Almighty inspired Bezaleel and Aholiab and other wise-hearted men to work cunningly for the tabernacle service, may we not think that printing was a divine inspiration! The tabernacle work was in time to pass away, but printing will last coeval with time. Several cities in olden time claimed the honour of being the birthplace of Homer, and several cities also claim to have been the seat of this unspeakable invention. The names of Gutenberg, Fust, Scheffer, Caxton, and others, the world will not willingly let die. By most accounts, John Gutenberg, of Mentz, in Germany, is credited with the invention, though Haarlem in Holland, coupled with the name of Laurence Koster, and Strasburg, have also those who favour their claim. Be that as it may, good old William Caxton brought the art of printing to England: all honour to him! Some of the books printed by him are to be found in the public libraries and among the collections of the nobility. Little did Caxton think, when in his sanctum at the old Abbey of Westminster, what a revolution would follow the introduction of printing! I think I may assert that the greatest changes the world has ever seen in the overturning of empires and dynasties by no means equal the mighty revolution effected by the power of the press; and we too, in our " tight little, snug little island" have been the largest recipients of the benefit. Mind you, the press was not always its own master. I lately read that a poor printer in Cloth Fair in the time of James the Second received a visit from one of the vile Government officials, accompanied by his officers. On getting into the house they found the printing - office all in confusion; the type had been made " pye " of, the sheets were scattered, and some carried over the walls to the next house. The poor man had been induced to print some sheets opposed to the King's Majesty, and the proof was too real to be denied. He was taken to prison, and from the prison to the judge, who pronounced on the unfortunate man a sentence not fit for decent ears. His cries for mercy were unheeded, and he suffered a cruel death.

About this time, writers gave to the books very singular titles. Some such titles are hardly fit to be repeated, while some may be named to show the strange conceits of the authors. I give a few such titles: *A handkerchief for Wet Eyes; A Pair of Bellows to blow off the dust cast upon John Fry; Hooks and Eyes for Believers' Breeches; A most delectable perfume for God's Saints to smell at; High-heeled shoes for Dwarfs in holiness; Crumbs of Comfort for the Chickens of the Covenant; A sigh of sorrow for the sinners of Sion breathed out of a hole in the wall of an earthen vessel; Seven sobs of a sorrowful soul for sin, or the seven penitential Psalms.*

There are some very readable books to be met with, containing anecdotes of authors, publishers, etc. I would name Disraeli's (father of Lord Beaconsfield) *Curiosities of Literature,* his *Quarrels and Calamities of Authors,* his *Amenities of Literature,* Spence's *Anecdotes of Men and Books,* and many others.

Think of the time when Bibles were chained

to reading - desks, so scarce were they. There
is a picture of " Bible Reading in Old St. Paul's "
Cathedral, beautifully described by the poet.

> Within the old cathedral dim
>   A solemn group are met,
> And hearts are glowing in their heat,
>   And cheeks with tears are wet.
> The Book is chainèd at the desk,
>   And from its page the throng
> Listen to Him of Nazareth,
>   Or Zion's holy song.

Before printing was invented, if a labouring man
wished to possess the Word of God, it would cost
him fifteen years of his earnings to enable him to
do so. You have probably heard the legend of
Dr. Faustus and the Devil. It appears that Fust
(or Faustus) carried the invention to Paris. At
first he sold his Bibles at the price of written ones,
then he reduced them one half, and afterwards
offered them for thirty crowns. This took the
people by surprise, and he was taken to prison and
put on his trial as a wizard. He then confessed
that he printed the books, and so saved his life.

Crabbe the poet sings—

> Books give
> New views to life and teach us how to live.
> They soothe the grieved, the stubborn they chastise,
> Fools they admonish and inform the wise.
> Their aid they yield to all; they never shun
> The man of sorrow, nor the wretch undone.
> Unlike the hard, the selfish and the proud,
> They fly not sullen from the suppliant crowd.
> Nor tell to various people various things,
> But show to subjects what they show to kings.

Let me give you an epitaph or two; one on Adam Wilkinson, of Edinburgh—a printer, no doubt—

"The volume of my life is finished, not without many errors; most of them have arisen from bad composition, and are to be attributed more to the case than to the press. There are also a great number of my own blotches, blurs, and bad register, but the True and Faithful Superintendent has undertaken to correct the whole. When the machine is again set up, incapable of decay, a new and perfect edition of my life will appear elegantly bound for duration, and every way fitted for the grand library of the Great Author."

I give another: "Here lies the remains of John Hulme, printer, who, like an old worn-out type, battered by frequent use, reposes in the grave, but not without a hope that at some future time he might be recast in the mould of righteousness, and safely locked up in the blissful chase of immortality."

Many will have read Benjamin Franklin's epitaph: "The body of Benjamin Franklin (like the cover of an old book, its contents worn out, and stript of its lettering and gilding) lies here, food for worms. Yet the work itself shall not be lost, for it will appear (as he believes) once more in a new and more beautiful edition, corrected and amended by the Author."

Milton received but £15 for his noble poem of

Paradise Lost, and Defoe received for his *Robinson Crusoe* probably as little, for it was refused by every bookseller, till one, more speculative than the rest, bought the copyright, and made £1000 by the sale. More than forty editions appeared in as many years. Compare these wretched payments with the princely sums paid by the house, say, of John Murray, who gave £23,540 to Lord Byron for his poems, from the years 1807 to 1823! Other houses have been equally liberal. A poem of two or three pages appeared a short time ago in the *Contemporary Review,* for which its author, Lord Tennyson, received a guinea a line!

A lady poet has written—

> Books! sweet associate of the silent hour,
>   What blessed inspiration do I owe
> To your companionship, your peaceful power
>   High and pure pleasure ever can bestow.
> Of noble ones I trace the path thro' life,
>   Joy in their joys, and sorrow as they mourn,
> Gaze on their Christian animating strife,
>   And shed some fond tears o'er their untimely end.
> Or with heroic beings tread the soil
>   Of a freed country by themselves made free,
> And taste the recompense of virtuous toil,
>   The exaltations of humanity.

I will now conclude in the words of Henry Ward Beecher, who says: "Books are the windows through which the soul looks out. A house without books is like a room without windows. No man has a right to bring up his children without surrounding them with books, if he has the means of buying them. It is a wrong to his family. He cheats them. Children learn to read by being in the presence of books. The love of knowledge comes with reading, and grows upon it. And the love of knowledge in a young mind is almost a warrant against the inferior excitement of passions and vices. . . . A library is not a luxury, but one of the necessaries of life."

The following poem (or rather part of one) is too good to be omitted in this talk on

OLD BOOKS

I must confess I love old books !
  The dearest, too, perhaps most dearly :
Thick, clumsy tomes, of antique looks,
  In pigskin covers fashioned queerly ;

Clasped, chained, or thonged, stamped quaintly too
  With figures, wondrous strange, of holy
Men and women, and cherubs, few
  Might well from owls distinguish duly.

I love black-letter books, that saw
  The light of day at least three hundred
Long years ago, and look with awe
  On works that live, so often plundered.

   .   .   .   .   .

To be enlightened, counselled, led
  By master minds of former ages,
Come to old books, consult the dead,
  Commune with silent saints and sages.

Dearly beloved old pigskin tomes
  Of dingy hue, old bookish darlings :
O, cluster ever round my room,
  And banish strife, disputes, and snarlings.

CHAPTER XIII

MEN I HAVE KNOWN

WHAT a goodly array of men pass through my memory as I collect materials for my closing chapter of these *Recollections*—men whose fame the Methodist world will not willingly let die. As one of the surviving preachers called out by our Founder, I think I should first name the truly venerable Richard Reece. He was our Superintendent at City Road, and at times occupied the Hackney Road pulpit. He was a grand old man, one that a stranger would not pass without looking at. His knee-breeches and shoe-buckles spoke of him as a man of a former century. His chief question to us youngsters, asked in tremulous tones, was, "Have you given your heart to God?" At a lovefeast at Hackney Road one good brother became rather prosy, when Mr. Reece stopped him, saying, "That will do, brother; now for another." I loved the old man, and was a bit of a favourite with him. He came out in 1786, and died in 1856.

Another of Mr. Wesley's men was the Rev.

Joseph Sutcliffe ; he was very aged and feeble when I knew him, and wore an old-fashioned cloak. His Commentary on the Bible was better known a generation ago than it is now. It is a truly valuable body of divinity. The first time I saw George Morley I was struck with his ponderosity. His good wife and he were much loved at Woodhouse Grove School, where they reigned for many years.

For Dr. Bunting I had much loving respect. I knew him in his vigour, and also in "age and feebleness extreme." I remembered what a great man he was among us, and respected him the more. He was always pleased to see me when I had to call on him at his house on business, and he has asked me never to pass his door without calling in to see him. The first volume of his " Life " was written by his son in 1859, and the concluding volume by the Rev. G. S. Rowe in 1887, after the long interval of twenty-eight years. The question asking when volume two would be ready, became a byword. It is reported that Mr. Bunting was with his guides engaged in climbing one of the Alps, and drawing near to another group of climbers he was startled by the shout: " When are you going to bring out that second volume ? " With Dr. Bunting I must associate his gifted son, W. M. Bunting. I was an occasional visitor to his house at Highgate Rise. Who does not remember his attenuated form, cased in coat

and scarf? He was a sadly afflicted man, and
I remember reading one of his letters published
in his " Memorials," full of pathos,—how his arch-
enemy the north-east wind got at him in his
chamber, in spite of every precaution taken to
keep it out I believe our beautiful Covenant
Service hymn, " O God, how often hath Thine ear,"
was written by him when very young. His
beloved wife survived him many years, and not
very long before her death offered a large selection
of her late husband's books to the Allan Library;
and it was my pleasurable task to make the
selection of about six hundred volumes, which
formed a valuable addition to those treasures.
Mrs. W. M. Bunting was a truly saintly woman.

MR. THOMAS MARRIOTT

was, in my humble judgment, the greatest collector
of Wesleyana. He no doubt inherited many valuable Wesley curios from his father, Mr. W. Marriott,
who was one of Wesley's executors. Being early
in the market, he no doubt secured many items
which he could not have done in after-years. Then,
again, he made such a good use of his Methodist
treasures. For some years every month's issue of
our Magazine contained an article from his pen.
In my young days these contributions were the
first things I read when I got the Magazine, and
have been for many years a reader of it. A collection of Mr. Marriott's articles would form a most

interesting volume on old Methodism. I remember the old gentleman coming occasionally to the Mission House. He left his choice collection to Dr. Osborn, who was also a rare collector. I supplied him with many items; for I was an early rummager for the Doctor.

MR. JAMES NISBET,

the eminent publisher, was a man highly respected by all right-thinking people. I once had the pleasure of an interview with him. Part of my work at the Mission House in far-back times was to collect subscriptions from a few tradesmen who had kindly engaged to receive such, and, on calling at his publishing house in Berners Street, was taken up to his office to receive what had been paid to him for our Society. There was nothing striking in the transaction, but it gave me the opportunity of seeing a man whose name I had long respected, for much of my early reading bore his name as publisher on the title-page. I had long been satisfied that anything issued from his house was safe reading, and much of my reading was influenced by the publisher's name. Old Thomas Tegg, a voluminous publisher of Cheapside, and William Baynes, of Paternoster Row, both of whom reprinted a large number of good books, the Puritans' works, and others, come flitting through my memory, as I have had to do business with them.

THE REV. DR. KNOWLES

was another dear old friend whom I had long known. Having tastes and pursuits so much in common, we were drawn to each other; and it was a real delight when occasionally he invited me to spend the week-end at Tonbridge Wells, when rare books and curiosities of all kinds formed the subject of much of our talk. The only drawback was when Mrs. Knowles appeared, soon after ten o'clock, with a candlestick, as a hint that it was time to retire. Why, we could have sat for hours longer. Shortly before the learned Doctor died, Mrs. Knowles told me that he wished her to send for me as to the disposal of his books, of which he had a good collection. The result of the sale was highly satisfactory to Mrs. Knowles, while I was pleased at being able to render this service to my friend's widow. In conversation Dr. Knowles was full of anecdotes, and many of his stories had reference to events with which he was more or less connected. One day he bought at a rag-shop a small vase for sixpence. Years after, on retiring, he had to provide a home for himself, including a stock of crockery. The dealer gladly gave him five pounds' worth for his sixpenny vase. He once showed me a perfect and beautiful black Wedgwood teapot which he bought in a village for two shillings and sixpence. He was offered ten pounds for it, but declined to part with it.

THE REV. LUKE TYERMAN

was a man to be envied for his vast collection
of Wesleyana, possibly such as had never been
brought together before.   He had long been
a collector, and in course of time became the
possessor of the Rev. James Everett's treasures.
Few men had such opportunities as Mr. Everett
enjoyed for gathering up such items.   In addition
to that, he was an ardent Methodist antiquarian.
He was early in the field, before it had become a passion to collect Wesley items.   One
evening, many years ago, Mr. Tyerman kindly
invited me to spend an evening with him at
his house in Clapham Park.   Needless to say
that on my part it was an evening of enjoyment.
He told me how he had acquired his treasures
from Mr. Everett—much in these words :—Wanting to consult a document which he knew to be
in Mr. Everett's possession, he called on him to
ask permission to see the paper.   "You know
you voted against me," said Mr. Everett, referring
to the time when he had been expelled from
the Connexion, in the Reform agitation, "but we
will let that pass."   However, he kindly allowed
him to make use of the paper there and then.
Mr. Tyerman, in course of the interview, offered
to purchase for £100 the entire collection, which
he saw was a very valuable one.   Mr. Everett
replied that he would consult his wife ; and, woman-

like, she replied "yes" to the offer. Mr. Tyerman, thinking Mr. Everett might be tempted to sell, the more so as he was by no means a rich man, had taken with him two or three light large bags, into which he swept his purchase after handing in the cheque. I have a faint recollection of Mr. Tyerman telling me that Mr. Everett regretted what he had done next day, but Mr. Tyerman held him to his bargain.

Few men would have made such a good use of these treasures as Mr. Tyerman did. He was one of our most painstaking writers. His extensive Life of Wesley in three thick volumes, of Whitefield in two volumes, of S. Wesley, sen., and of Fletcher, was a good life's work. In his earlier years he was much in request for special services. His ministry lasted from 1844 to 1889.

THE REV. DANIEL J. DRAPER

Well do I remember that morning early in January 1866, when the news reached us at the Mission House of the loss of the *London*, in which nearly all perished, including the Rev. D. J. and Mrs. Draper, in the Bay of Biscay. Mr. Boyce walked about his room fairly distraught, for he and Mr. Draper were like brothers. We little thought, when he bade us good-bye a few days before, what a fearful disaster was hanging over him. After leaving London they had a succession of bad weather, culminating in the foundering of the good ship with its living freight. A small boat-load only reached land, as by a miracle. The ship was commanded by Captain Martin, one of the best mercantile captains afloat. The incidents afterwards told by survivors were truly affecting,—how earnestly Mr. Draper addressed his fellow-voyagers and the crew, entreating them to come to Christ. Doubtless, many found mercy at that eleventh hour. Mrs. Draper, too, pleaded with the passengers, and threw her cloak to one in the boat as they were pushing off.

A few days before leaving, Mr. Draper wrote to me to get him a copy of Bloomfield's *Farmer's Boy*, a book he read in his early days, and wanted to read again—a thorough English book, to be read in the fields on a summer's evening. I need not say how I prized his letter. I suggested to Mr. Smithies that the loss of the *London* would form an interesting number for the *Band of Hope Review*, which he adopted, giving a portrait, with scenes of the wreck, etc. What an unfathomable mystery it appeared to us! He entered the ministry in 1834. His was a truly valuable missionary life.

MR. JAMES NICHOLS, PRINTER

In this very nice old gentleman one had the *beau ideal* of one who lived more than a century ago. He printed for the Mission House for many years, so that I was much in contact with him. He was a *learned* printer, and there were few better

Latin scholars. Among his works he translated and printed the works of Arminius in two thick octavos : this was an immense undertaking, done in 1825; and it was not till 1875 that his son finished the work by translating and printing the third volume, a long interval between the beginning and ending of such a work. Other books on the Calvinistic controversy were issued by him. Of books and pamphlets, Methodist and otherwise, he printed a very large number.

His son William, who inherited much of his father's genius, died suddenly not long since. It was but two days before that event that we shook hands together. Our friendship had been a life-long one. I remember when he left school to take part in his father's business as a printer in Hoxton Square, and I see him now in memory perched up at his father's high desk reading proofs. With other works, he helped his father in editing the *Morning Exercises*, in six volumes—a popular work fifty years ago.

THE REV. WILLIAM MOISTER

was a missionary to the backbone. I never knew such a missionary man. He gave his long life to advance the Society's Missions, and to extend his Master's Kingdom. He wrote more missionary works than anyone I knew. The profits he gave away. He built the parsonage at Sedbergh, saving the Society there the annual rent of the preacher's house for ever. He invariably sent me his books, to write a notice of for our papers. When the Bradford Conference of 1878´was over, he kindly took me home with him to Sedbergh, and a most delightful little holiday it was. The master boat-man, a friend of Mr. Moister, rowed us about the lovely Windermere lake for an hour or two. This pleasure still lingers in my memory.

THE REV. WILLIAM ARTHUR, M.A.

My recollections of Mr. Arthur commenced in 1838, when he was a student at Hoxton Academy. He occasionally preached at Hackney Road, then the old Middlesex Chapel. In 1839 he went to the Mysore. His health, however, failed him, and he returned after a short service of three years. One result of his work in India was a series of articles in the *Methodist Magazine*, entitled " A Mission to the Mysore," afterwards published in book form. It was his first work, and showed that he possessed remarkable powers of descriptive writing. I leave to other pens to describe his work in City Road, Paris, Boulogne, Great Queen Street, Hinde Street, etc. He was in Paris during the Revolution of 1848, and gave his experience in a lecture. He was always a welcome lecturer before the Young Men's Christian Association, whose first lectures were given in the large room of the Centenary Hall. On his Mission House appointment I was brought much in contact with him, and a very friendly acquaintance was the result. I found that I was somewhat of a favourite, and was always called "Dear Thomas" in his letters to me. When he went to live at East Acton, he desired me to arrange his library. After that he went to Belfast, and, on his return, his library, which in the meantime had doubled, was a more formidable task to arrange and catalogue. It was, however, done to his complete satisfaction. On the lease of his Clapham house expiring, Mr. Arthur went to reside in the south of France, at Cannes, and the work of packing up his library, which looked so noble in the beautiful room in which it was located, was placed in my hands. He told me he intended taking another house in London, and would require his books, but, beyond the comparatively few he took with him, he never saw his beloved books again. He intimated to me not long since that the Allan Library would be their destination. A pleasing incident connected with *The Tongue of Fire* comes to my mind. His amanuensis, a warm-hearted Irishman, told me that when Mr. Arthur gave him the closing paragraph of that work he rose from his seat and crossed over to Mr. Arthur, gripped his hand, and said that generations to come would bless him for such words of inspiration. On the death of my wife he wrote me a most loving and brotherly letter of sympathy. Referring to Mrs. Arthur's death a few years before, he added, "And I am to the margin come." Mrs. Arthur's death was a great blow to him. She had a long and wearisome illness. I was at the house shortly before her death, and she expressed a wish to see me. I found her lying on a low sofa, and had to kneel down to catch her whispered words. With my young family I was a welcome visitor at times to East Acton and Clapham Common, with their beautiful gardens and orchards.

THE REV. SAMUEL J. STONE

Respecting this beautiful poet I sent the following to the *Methodist Recorder* soon after his decease. Dr. Rigg kindly expressed his pleasure with it:—

"'Weary of Earth, and Laden with my Sin.'— The author of this truly beautiful hymn (No. 794 in our Hymn-book), the Rev. S. J. Stone, has just passed to his eternal rest, after much pain and suffering, borne with true patience and resignation, aged sixty-one years. He was born in Staffordshire, educated at the Charterhouse (where he died); entered Pembroke College, Oxford, with an Exhibition; became curate at Windsor, but soon left to assist his father, as his curate, at St. Paul's, Haggerston, and eventually succeeded him as vicar. During his labours there he won the love of all his people, especially the young, and, when he left a few years ago to go to All Hallows, London Wall, deep regret was felt. He has left behind a loving memory. Besides the above, he was the author of many sweet hymns and poems; and the Thanksgiving Ode on the Prince of Wales's recovery from his almost fatal illness, which so deeply stirred the country, was written by Mr. Stone. It was sung at St. Paul's Cathedral, and in most of the churches in the United Kingdom. I have very pleasant recollections of him; he was so friendly and willing to serve anyone. One visit to my house, opposite to the Vicarage, in Broke Road, I well remember. It was to comfort and pray with my beloved father-in-law, an old Hackney Road Methodist, then near his end. As we knelt together he repeated this hymn with great earnestness and devotion, and I thought it most appropriate, there being so much of prayer in it. On one occasion the Rev. William Arthur asked me if I could find him a poem called 'The Rationalistic Chicken.' As I knew that Mr. Stone was its author, I called on him, and he obligingly gave me several copies for Mr. Arthur. It was written for an illustration depicting a chicken, just emerged from its shell, who would not believe that it had just come out of it, as it could not understand how it was. It was a clever rebuke for those who will not believe what they do not understand."

THE REV. DR. PUNSHON

The scene was Exeter Hall, filled with a congregation to the full, on the tiptoe of expectation, for Mr. Punshon was about to lecture before the Young Men's Christian Association on "John Bunyan." I was there with a fellow-clerk. Perfect silence reigned when the orator commenced, so that not a word might be lost. His lectures were always more largely attended than any others. As the oratory rolled forth, what varied emotions followed! We sat with bated breath, and now and then looked at each other with wonderment. But when the peroration came, such a bursting forth of cheers I never witnessed. That utterance, in my judgment, was one of the great orations of the world. I want the Rev. T. M'Cullagh's descriptive powers to show forth the splendour of his intimate friend's lecture. If I had paid a guinea for admission it would have been money well spent, for the memory of that lecture and its associations abide with me still. It was not the only lecture I heard Dr. Punshon give, but that in my judgment was his grandest, though, when talking with him and Mrs. Punshon about it years afterwards, he did not think it was his best. Mrs. Punshon regretted she had not heard it.

In course of time Dr. Punshon came to the Mission House as Missionary Secretary, and afterwards was appointed Deputy Treasurer. It was my privilege to act under him in receiving and banking the Society's receipts. Now and then he took me home to tea and to spend an evening among his autographs, of which he had a choice collection, the taste for which he occasionally indulged in amidst such a busy life as rarely falls to the lot of man. When Mr. Boyce left his house, *Tranby*, at Brixton Hill, Dr. Punshon took it of him, and it was my pleasure to arrange the Doctor's books on the shelves so well filled by Mr. Boyce's treasures, and afterwards to begin the catalogue, which his death stopped. This pleasant life, at least on my part, was too good to last. Disease laid hold of his well-built form, and took him from us. I doubt if Brixton ever witnessed such a funeral as was given to the deceased. I was one of the Mission House staff to follow his remains to Norwood Cemetery. I was ten weeks his senior, I found, when comparing ages.

I sent the following to the *Methodist Recorder*, and I am sure I shall be excused for its insertion here:—

" *To the Editor of the 'Methodist Recorder.'*

" DEAR SIR,—I cannot forbear, while the memory of our beloved senior Secretary is still fresh upon us, and when the tears shed by us for him are still undried, to add this expression of the love and esteem which myself and fellow-clerks at this House cherish for the memory of the late Dr. Punshon. Not only did we respect him for his brilliant powers as a public speaker, of which some of us were

witnesses in his early days, but we also respected
him for his stern integrity, deep insight, and devotion to the cause of our Missions—a cause which
was ingrained in his very being.   His duties were
not mere perfunctory ones, for he made himself
thoroughly informed of every detail of his treasurer-
ship.   Not a cheque would he sign without well
knowing the reason for its being drawn.   His
acquaintance with his work was *thorough*.   All
this won respect from us.   The inadequacy of the
Society's income to meet its expenditure was a
source of deep anxiety to him.   If the morning's
post brought but a small sum to the Society's funds
his concern was visible, but a good day's remit-
tance was a source of real joy to him, and, when
occasionally a handsome donation came to hand,
the formal acknowledgment was invariably accompanied by words from his pen of special thankfulness.   It was a painful task to him to have to
borrow so often from our bankers large sums of
money, to meet the incessant demands made upon
us as bills became due.   He made the Mission
cause his own, and how deeply he was devoted to
his work is well known.   His was a large diocese,
embracing correspondence with the officials of the
Australian and Canadian Conferences, together with
France, Germany, Italy, and Spain.   Some of the
European stations he occasionally visited.   His
last day here is well remembered : on leaving he
shook hands with us and gave us his best wishes.

Little did we think that we would see his face no more. He is now serving the Great Master in heaven, whom he served so well on earth. Costly wreaths were laid on his coffin, but he has laid on our hearts a precious wreath of loving memory which we shall ever cherish.—I am, Sir, yours respectfully, for self and fellow-clerks,

"THOMAS HAYES.

"WESLEYAN MISSION HOUSE,
"BISHOPSGATE STREET WITHIN, *April* 25."

MR. T. B. SMITHIES

Who did not love this good man? One was drawn to him almost at first sight; and what a life of loving usefulness he lived! He was often at the Mission House on Committees and other business. For a long time he was head of the firm publishing the *British Workman* and a host of other highly valuable books and publications. He was always full of work and good deeds. The animal world found in him a very powerful advocate, and he was a true lover of humanity. His publications show this. On the occasion of a trip I made to Holland, he kindly sent to me a good bundle of the *British Workman,* in Dutch, to distribute on my journey, and he was pleased with the report I gave him. At a public meeting at the Mission House, with which I had to do, he spoke of me in a way too flattering to repeat.

THE REV. W. B. BOYCE

My earliest recollection of Mr. Boyce was in 1843, when he returned to England from the chairmanship of the Graham's Town District; and a more vivid remembrance when, two years later, he left England to take charge of the Australian Missions. The events connected with his departure are well remembered by me. I see in imagination the busy little man, as full of activity as he ever was, making every preparation for the comfort of his beloved wife and four little daughters,— afterwards Lady Allen, wife of Sir Wigram Allen; Mrs. Alexander M'Arthur; Mrs. J. H. Stewart, of Bathurst; and Mrs. Gibson, of Paris. The morning of their departure was a lively one, and a large gathering of friends and officials saw them off. I little thought then that my acquaintance with him would ripen into such a life-long friendship— nay, till even after his death, for a valuable book gift reached me after he had been dead a few weeks, the parcel being addressed by him very shortly before his death.

In 1856 he returned to England, and gladly was he welcomed after an absence of eleven years. Then in time came his appointment to the Mission House as one of the General Secretaries. Of his Mission House life I can but say that it was a pleasure to us all. He showed very little of the *master* but much of the *friend*, as he was to us

all. For many years I was his clerk, sitting
with him in his room, for he liked me to be there.
No one rendered more willing service than I did
to my good friend. I may say these were the
happiest days of my life. There was scarcely a
subject on which I asked for information—for he
encouraged me to ask—but he could supply it.
And he was always a learner himself. No locality
he read of in book or newspaper but he was
bound to find where it was by reference to his
large atlas, always at band. His knowledge of
geography was most extensive; and soon after
he went to Australia he issued a small school-
book on that science. His ready wit was amusing,
and one seldom got the better of him, and his
replies were ever ready. It was a treat to hear
at times his clever repartees with some of his
choice friends who occasionally called at the Mission
House.

One Monday morning he asked me who I heard
preach the day before. I replied that though I
heard the preacher I knew nothing of the sermon,
for my head was filled with the pounds, shillings,
and pence of the Annual Report I was then carrying
through the press. I remember asking him why
we had not the power given to us to shut out
such wanderings. He replied that, if we possessed
that power, we should shut out what we ought
to remember. I thought there was much wisdom
in his reply.

I went occasionally to his beautiful house on Brixton Hill, to help arrange his books, etc. He had a way of his own, which in my humble judgment was perfect. His library was a sight. Every book was in nice condition, and the shelves of the large room extended all round it. Now and then came a weeding time, much to my benefit.

Mr. Boyce's office-work did not end when he left to go home. Often has he brought a batch of letters in the morning, which had occupied him all the evening before, on business matters. His despatch of business was remarkable, and so was his insight into details. His life was a busy one, as may be gathered from what I have said. I believe most of the reviews of books in the *Watchman*, and many in the *Methodist Recorder*, were written by him, sometimes extending to two or three columns. His leaving the Mission House, after being with us eighteen years, was a sad event to us all. Twice afterwards he visited England, to the joy of his friends and relatives.

His last visit was to see again his children and grandchildren; also to carry through the press his last and great work, the result of a lifetime of historical reading and study: *An Introduction to the Study of History; Civil, Ecclesiastical, and Literary*—a portly octavo volume of 668 pages. It will remain a standing memorial of his extraordinary powers of reading and condensation.

His friendship for me he continued to my young married daughter on her arrival in Sydney; and he dedicated her first-born to the Almighty by baptism.

I sent the following extract from Fronde's *Oceana* to the *Methodist Recorder*, thinking it such an appropriate tribute to my dear old friend:—— " The person whom I liked best was Lady Allen's father, a beautiful old clergyman of eighty-two, who told me that he had read all my books; that he disapproved deeply of much that he found in them, but that he had formed, notwithstanding, a sort of regard for the writer. He followed me into the hall when we went away, and gave me his blessing. Few gifts have ever been bestowed on me in this world which I have valued more. Sir Wigram Allen, I regret to see, is since dead: the life and spirits which were flowing over so freely that night, all now quenched and silent. He could not have had a better friend near him at the moment of departure than that venerable old man."

SIR WM. M'ARTHUR, K.C.M.G.

I had the pleasure and privilege of Sir Wm. M'Arthur's friendship for some years. It was through his brother-in-law, Mr. Boyce, that I became known to Mr. M'Arthur, as he then was. In time he made me his librarian, and this brought me much into contact with him. His library was a very fine one, not only for its contents, but for the nice condition the books were in, and the handsome mahogany shelves on which they rested. He was particular as to the cataloguing, so that a book might be found at once. And he was so pleasant to be with. I was able to give him my Saturdays. His niece, Miss M'Millan, was his amanuensis; and Saturdays were always busy days, much of his correspondence being done on that day. His business habits greatly helped him in the despatch of his correspondence.

During Sir William's mayoralty he twice honoured me with invitations to dine with him at the Mansion House—once with the provincial mayors of England, in their robes and gold chains, and a grand sight it was; and once in private. His sudden death was a great blow to Methodism, for which he spared neither purse nor person to serve. His excellences are well set forth in the beautiful Memoir of him written by his friend, the Rev. T. M'Cullagh, to whom I sent a few jottings respecting his library, which he inserted in it, as follows:—" Of the library itself, and of Sir William in it, Mr. Hayes says, 'It was good and useful, and largely a reference library. The most prominent works were named. He would sometimes repeat passages to me from memory, giving them in good style. . . . Too much time was spent with his correspondence, and I often urged him to spare himself, and enjoy his books more; and this he was always hoping to do. . . . He was always pleased to tell me of his day's work, which for extent and variety was marvellous,' " etc.

My connection with the M'Arthur family has been a long and interesting one, and was not broken off with Sir William's death. I have still charge of the beloved library. Mr. A. M'Arthur, with Mrs. M'Arthur and their family, have shown me much kindness, including Mrs. and Miss M'Millan, sister and niece of Sir William.

THE REV. WM. GIBSON, B.A.

I was pleased to include Mr. Gibson among my dear friends. His smiling face was always a pleasure to see. His work in Paris often brought him to the Mission House. I shall not soon forget the kindness he and Mrs. Gibson showed to me when on a visit to the French capital. On one of Mr. Boyce's visits to England he said I had rendered him so much useful service that he would like me to go to Paris at his expense. Needless to say I enjoyed my trip, greatly furthered by Mr. Gibson's advice how to make the most of it, giving me lists of places to visit. It was while wandering near the huge castle of Vincennes that I was warned off by the guard. I did not think I had much the look of a spy about me. It was a pleasure to go to some of the services, at one of which I was asked to speak, the missionary in charge being my interpreter. I sent at the time an account of what I saw of Methodism to the *Recorder*

Of Mr. and Mrs. Gibson's work in Paris, " the day will declare it "; it was truly a noble work, one not to be tabulated. Seed was sown, resulting in many, very many French folk receiving Christ. And so did many an Englishman who attended our services there. The siege of Paris, and still more the Commune, were terrible times for our good friends. I remember how very anxious Mr. Boyce was about his daughter and her family.

A Mission boat did good service on the various rivers. On one occasion Mr. Gibson told me he saw a crowd on the wharf after an evening service, and, on looking to see what it meant, he found that his wife was speaking for Jesus from the boat deck to the bystanders on the shore.

Mr. Gibson's death was a severe loss to our work in Paris, of which he, with his excellent wife, was the life and soul. His ministry extended from 1852 to 1894.

There are other names I love to dwell upon, but the foregoing must suffice. I wish I had kept a diary of my early life : what an interesting panorama of events it would have been ! But what boy keeps a journal ? I have had to depend chiefly on my memory for these jottings.

" Friend after friend departs," and in my peaceful

eventide it has been an anticipation of reunion above, to recall the memory of these companions of life's day.

In bringing these *Recollections* to a close, I trust I shall be pardoned for inserting the following communication inserted in the *Methodist Recorder* of January 23, 1902 :—

"A VISIT TO A METHODIST ANTIQUARIAN

" Mr. William Page writes from Dalston :—

" Hearing that one of your occasional contributors, and a dear old friend of my own, Mr. Thomas Hayes, formerly of the Mission House and the Allan Library, was laid aside by illness, I called upon him a few days ago, and found him temporarily disabled by rheumatism, but, under the loving care of his daughters, as cheery and hopeful as ever. Not only so, but he was busy preparing for publication some of the recollections of his long connection with Methodism—a work which I think will have attractions for many readers of the *Recorder*. An ardent antiquarian and zealous Methodist, he has managed to gather a fine collection of Wesleyana, and he was at work surrounded by busts, portraits, medallions, pottery, pictures, letters, books, etc., all relating to the venerable Founder of Methodism, for whom he entertains the greatest admiration and respect. At the same time, his passion for collecting has not been restricted to Wesleyan items, for his museum includes idols from the East and South, savage ornaments and weapons, and numerous curiosities from missionary fields of labour. Another feature is an unusually large collection of the celebrated oil-prints of the late George Baxter. Mr. Hayes tells me that he long enjoyed the friendship of this artist, and that he always took a great interest in his publications. Mr. Baxter's method was of his own invention, and as I inspected the various pictures I could not help wondering, with Mr. Hayes, why a process that had such excellent results was allowed to fall into desuetude when the publisher - artist died. Mr. Hayes, I find, has also managed to accumulate some thousands of engravings, woodcuts, portraits, biblical illustrations, and specimens of the work of Cruikshank, Gustave Doré, and others, while his books not only fill entirely one large room, but are packed away in every corner of the house where space can be spared, and even occupy the summer-house in the garden. I trust Mr. Hayes will be long spared to arrange and enjoy his treasures, and to send occasionally some little jottings to the *Recorder.*"

PRINTED BY MORRISON AND GIBB LIMITED, EDINBURGH

CPSIA information can be obtained at www.ICGtesting.com
Printed in the USA
LVOW06s0146141115

462582LV00033B/1551/P